LOVE STRATEGIES

The book for everyone who cares about the relationship they
have, or hope to achie

LOVE Strategies

Successful Relationships —
What Makes Them Work
and How *YOURS* Can be One

Ian Grove-Stephensen and Susan Quilliam

THORSONS PUBLISHING GROUP
Wellingborough, Northamptonshire

•

Rochester, Vermont

First published 1987

British Library Cataloguing in Publication Data

Grove-Stephensen, Ian
Love strategies: successful relationships:
what makes them work and how yours can
be one.
1. Couples
I. Title   II. Quilliam, Susan
306.7   HQ799.95

ISBN 0-7225-1324-0

Printed and bound in Great Britain

Contents

Dedication

For each other

Acknowledgements

Our thanks to everyone who has made this book possible, including all the individuals and couples who gave us the benefit of their experience, and particularly:

Trevor Day, Kevin and Tracey Donaghue, Caroline Fruin and Surya, John and Julia Howard, Syed Bodrul Islam and Salma Bodrul, Sue Linge, John Masters and Caroline Thorpe, Mary O'Dowd, David Roberts and Jo Spence, Ivan Sokolov and Jacquie Pearson, and Jane and Steve Yelding.

Introduction

Love strategies are ways of learning to love. No one ever teaches you how to make a relationship work. There are no evening classes, no correspondence courses, and no sixteen-plus exams in what is perhaps the most vital area of most people's lives; the art of making, keeping — and if necessary breaking — the relationships that make their lives worth living.

Despite all this, even in our age of high divorce rates, some people do make their relationships work successfully for them. People do fall in love, they do find someone that suits them. They do have good sex. There are happy marriages, some of which last for a lifetime. And there are relationships which end successfully, with each partner having gained a lot before being ready to move on.

So there must be a way of making things work. But what is it? What ways, what strategies do people use for relationship success? And how can we pass them on? These were the questions we were asking ourselves two years ago, when the idea for this book first came to us.

We had started out with varied histories. Sue had already had a long-term relationship when she met Ian. Ian had had an on-off relationship which had included a living-together phase, and had since had a number of friendships which included sex. From the beginning of our own relationship, we had come face to face with the very real issue of how to make two extremely strong-minded individuals into a functioning whole without murder or compromise!

We were also concerned that as far as we could see, all around us were intelligent, happy people who were struggling to make relationships work simply because they didn't know how to go about it. We wondered what would happen if these people suddenly got successful... and made successful couples... which led to a successful society. Now there was a thought!

We had a number of resources to help us. We've each done a lot of Cocounselling, a self-help support method that encourages you to change by expressing and celebrating your feelings and thoughts. We've also both studied Neuro-Linguistic Programming, a new language in the science of psychology, that allows you to work with what goes on in your own mind to change the way you think and feel about things.

Using these ways of looking at the world, our first step was to go in search of success. Were there, in fact, individuals out there who were able to enter, develop or leave relationships in a way that worked? If not, it was back to the drawing board...

We found some. We talked to all sorts of people; couples married for forty years, single people happy being alone, new couples, old couples, couples in arranged marriages, individuals who talked to us about successful partings, ecstatic cohabitees, and euphoric bed-hoppers.

It wasn't all sweetness and light. We didn't find anyone who never rowed, and some of the couples we interviewed have since split up. What we did find were lots of people who, in their definition of the word (not ours), had elements in their relationships that worked and were successful. And although we were in no sense of the word doing a statistical survey, we also found that many couples did things which were, broadly speaking, similar. They used similar approaches, similar strategies for making love work.

But was it possible to pass any of this on? Or did the things that worked for these people only work for them? To test this out, we did a few things. We worked, in our psychotherapy practice, with people who had relationship difficulties. We tried suggesting that they do some of the things that our interviewees did, to see if they worked. We also ran three weekend workshops on what we had learned. Sometimes we fell flat on our faces, trying to pass on knowledge or experience in inappropriate ways. Sometimes we really helped.

All the time, often painfully, we kept on at our relationship, trying out things, adapting things, working things out. And somehow, in among the brainstorms, the interviews, the papers spread over the lounge floor, the rows and the hugs, we got a book.

What is the book? We've tried to examine the strategies that people use that make relationships work; how they experience the world, how they think, how they feel, how they behave in a way that seems to make for success. Sometimes these strategies are very different from each other. Sometimes they are the same. We've presented them from the viewpoint of our past experience and our models, although we're sure you will find your own ways to understand what we are saying. We've structured each section so that, particularly if you use the explorations we've included, you get the strategy, and ways to use it yourself, not just an account of what other people do. We've aimed to offer you real skills you can use in your own situation to make or break a relationship, as well as to improve one.

So what is the book not? It's certainly not the answer to a perfect relationship. We didn't find anyone who said they had that, and in any case we're suspicious of books that claim to change your life.

Nor is this book a series of lectures by experts on what to do or not to do, or even a series of too-good-to-be-true interviews with soft-focus couples who claim to have got it totally right. We're not experts, and neither were our interviewees; if something we say doesn't work for you, drop it and try something else.

This book isn't a statistical survey; couples who claim to be successful don't break down into neatly defined groups. We did talk to a wide variety of people, but we are aware that some of the things we seemed to discover may not apply to all sections of society. Cultures where arranged marriages are the norm, for example, may not produce relationships like many of the ones we described, although we did talk to representatives of these cultures, and found that many things they said were useful for this book.

We don't concentrate too much on specific problems, like money, sex, who does the housework. What we found in the interviews was that very often the specific problem in a relationship wasn't all that important. It was the way it was handled that made the difference between a successful couple and one that saw itself as failing. Money might be a worry for two sets of partners, but the way that worry was handled could vary dramatically. So when you read about different strategies, you can apply them to any of the areas of difficulty in your life.

One specific area we aren't concentrating on is children. Many of the people we interviewed, single people and couples alike, had children, and we know that a relationship changes when it involves other people, whatever their role is. But we felt the book could develop into a ten-volume series if it took into account variations on the family situation!

Having got a clear idea of what we're aiming to do in the book, you are probably wondering about the way it's organized. In fact, the organization came about by putting hundreds of pieces of paper on the lounge floor, and then pushing them about from one position to the other! And what we came up with was this.

There is love, and there are strategies for love. Everyone we talked to made this distinction. So our first chapter sets the scene by explaining what love can mean, the wide variety of thoughts, feelings and behaviours that can be included in that one word. We also explain what we mean by strategies and how to use them, so that before you begin to explore them, you have the basics.

From Chapter 2 onwards, we offer you strategies. There are eighteen of them, collected in chapter groups according to roughly where you need them in a relationship. But there is a great deal of cross-over, and a strategy you need at the start, such as negotiation, may well be used throughout a relationship, even down to negotiating a parting.

So in general you will find that the early strategies in the book deal with the early stages of a relationship — even to considering what happens before you meet someone, for the situation you are in, the past you bring with you, and the person that you are, all affect the relationships you have (Love Strategies 1-3). We also look at what you want from a relationship, and how you go about choosing a partner in the first place (Love Strategies 4-5), both of which can be vital to how things work out.

Once in a relationship, there are many things to be thought about. Possibly the first consideration is the process of getting close to your partner and forging links (Love Strategies 6-8). Then, you each work towards what you want in the situation, giving and taking, maybe needing to negotiate in order to make it work (Love Strategies 9-10).

For us, the central issue in a relationship is the balance between you as the individual and you as part of a partnership. Getting this right seems to be the key issue in making love work.

We've included references to this throughout the book, but two particular love strategies cover the pull between what you as an individual want and what being part of a relationship demands (Love Strategies 11-12).

Of course there can be problems, and again these possibilities are dealt with throughout the book. We have also devoted one whole Chapter to how to handle crises (Love Strategy 13).

If the problems don't resolve themselves, you may need to think about leaving, and once you've decided, make the leaving work (Love Strategies 14-15). If the problems do resolve themselves, then you are ready to look to the future, set goals, commit yourself more fully — maybe even making long-term love work as the fulfilment of your life (Love Strategies 16-18).

This then is the form of the book. Each strategy has its own form. It contains the ways of thinking, feeling and behaving that we have discovered are vital. We've explained what we found out, sometimes using models from our own theoretical background, and always including parts of the interviews or conversations that gave us the knowledge, sometimes as quotations, sometimes as representative comments. We have included opportunities for you to explore your own situation, step by step, asking questions about yourself and your present or prospective relationships. These explorations will not only tell you about yourself, and so help you to work out what to do in the future. They also start you off using the strategy that we've been talking about, so you can apply it to your life.

You may notice, as you read the book, that there are pictures, as well. They're mainly there just for you to enjoy.

How do you use this book, now you've got it? The first thing to remind you of is that you don't have to be in a relationship to read this book. It's for people who want to improve their ability to get into relationships — and get out of them too!

You don't have to force your partner to read the book too. In fact it's best if you don't. If your partner really wants to read the book, to swap thoughts and feelings about it, that's fine; we've usually included suggestions for how to work together to get the most out of the explorations. But you can influence and improve your relationship on your own. And if you need extra support to get what you want, a stamped addressed envelope to us care of the publisher will bring you a list of resources, including details of our own therapy and counselling practice.

Read this book in a way you enjoy. Read the whole thing from cover to cover, or just browse. Do the explorations one after another, or in the order that suits you. If you learn just one thing from the book, it will affect the way you think and behave, maybe not immediately, but certainly in the long-term. For you too can learn to love. You can learn to choose partners who are right for you, and whom you are right for. You can learn to find out and negotiate for what you want. When crises strike, you can learn to overcome the anger, the frustration and the boredom, and work round or through the problems. You can learn to get out when it's right, and stay with it when that's right. You can use all your intelligence, power and caring to create a loving future. You too can be a Love Strategist!

Note:
For ease of reading, we have tended to use personal pronouns alternately, rather than him/her each time. Please read he for she and vice versa, particularly when working on the Explorations — all questions are meant for each of you.

1.

Love Strategies: the basics

Before learning any new skill, you need to know the basics. This Chapter gives you the basic knowledge you need in order to be able to apply love strategies to your relationship. It explains first of all what we mean by a successful strategy, then what we found out about what love itself means. Finally, we offer some guidelines about beginning to use the strategies.

What are Love Strategies?
In the days when you married someone from your own village, or at furthest the one ten miles across the valley, love wasn't such a big event. You looked around and saw couples courting, marrying and starting families. You had intimate knowledge of your own parents' interactions, rows and negotiations — and often, given the size of many village houses, intimate knowledge of their love-making too. You saw exactly how other people ran relationships — how they communicated, supported, got what they wanted. And, as children often do, you picked out the best bits, and copied them when you began your own relationship.

Nowadays, when most people disappear into their semis at six o'clock, to reappear only on the commuter trains in the morning, we don't have all these experiences. We literally don't learn how to love in the same detail as our ancestors did. Most of us find out the hard way, by trial and error. Often, error.

So, whether starting, ending or running a relationship, we often know what to do — find and be happy with a partner — but are a little less clear about how to do it. We know how to ride a bike, make a phone call, even conduct a tricky business meeting, because we have developed the strategies for doing these things. We know the process, the right state of mind, the mental steps we need to go through. No one ever teaches us the strategies we need to make relationships successful.

Let's be clear about what we mean by a strategy. The dictionary describes it as a plan of campaign; we prefer to think about it as a way of experiencing, thinking, feeling and behaving that allows you to do things as effectively as possible. Love, for example.

We all learn and use strategies all the time. We learn a strategy called reading which allows us to think in a certain way in order to understand marks on paper. We learn a strategy called enthusiasm which allows us to feel approving, and maybe even excited, when something happens that we like. As children, we don't have these strategies; we learn them as we grow, by watching, learning and practising.

Strategies are about process, not content. Reading, for example, is a strategy that is useful whatever the content, be it *Noddy in Toyland* or the Stock Market prices. Enthusiasm can be a good strategy whether you're reacting to a new dress or an old friend. Strategies are about the approaches you have to things — the mental processes, the emotional states, the ways of behaving that you need in order to get things done.

And what about Love Strategies? These again are about the way you do things, not about what you do. So we won't be suggesting which restaurant you go to in order to fall in love all over again; but we may be covering strategies to decide on the right restaurant for both of you. There's no point in our telling you to make love in a certain position; but we can certainly suggest strategies for you and your partner to communicate about the positions you want. And it doesn't really matter whether you row about fidelity or the vacuum cleaner — the same strategies for resolving that row will be useful.

Every person we talked to had some strategies which they used in their relationships. They had ways of going about things, experiencing, thinking, feeling and behaving, which affected their success. Many of them weren't aware of their strategies, but they still used them to get back together after a row, to go for what they really wanted, to negotiate a parting that was right for both of them. 'We very quickly learned that Lynn after work was a very different person from Lynn at weekends, and developed ways to handle that. . .' (Alex)

The strategies we tell you about in the book are the best ones we've found. Not everyone we talked to used every strategy we mention, but every strategy we describe has been used and refined by at least one successful couple. If you like, it's been road-tested!

So what do we mean by success? The success of the glowing bride and groom, entering with breathless anticipation on their life together? The success of the older couple, catching each other's glance across the room to pass that wordless communication that only seems to be possible after the golden wedding celebrations? Or maybe by success we mean something far more low-key — the satisfaction of waking in the morning to find that, yes, you are beside the right person, and the fact that he needs to clean his teeth doesn't matter one bit.

In fact, we mean all of these, and none of them. For success, we discovered, is a very personal thing. We interviewed couples who defined success by their ability to talk to each other, and others who considered the relationship only achieved its five-star rating after several extremely painful years of marriage. For us, the day we finally agreed that our own personal and very real resentments around housework were worth resolving in order to make the relationship work was the day we realized that we might possibly have enough motivation to make it a success. We still mark the degree of progress we've made in love by the number of days the draining board stays pristine.

Success in love can even survive partings. Some of the most congruent descriptions of success we've heard came from people who had loved and been loved — and left. 'It doesn't matter that it's over now,' said Dan, thinking back to a two-year relationship that ended by mutual consent, 'We both got what we wanted, had a good time, and then decided it was time to move on. No problem.' Even if the issues aren't as clear-cut as these, even if you are the 'left' rather than the leaver, bulk-buys of Kleenex and very real self-doubt can be superseded, given time, by real satisfaction with the experience and the knowledge that you did learn and gain. In that sense, many people can look back and realize that on its own terms, a past relationship was not a failure at all.

So what about you? In this book, you will read about a variety of relationships. Some you'll identify with, some will leave you cold. But the main point of the book is not for you to learn about other people's success; it is for you to have some success of your own. And you might like, even at this point, to allow your mind to drift off to what *you* want. To have a relationship? To have a different relationship? To be free of the one you're in? To have exactly the same relationship, except with not quite so many late-night rows, with a lot more afternoon cuddles, or a whole lot more eye-to-eye communication.

You may be very happy with the strategies you use to get the success you want in the relationship you want. Or you may want some new strategies, and some of your old ones may need updating, refining, retuning. If so, there's no need to hang on to them. Have one of ours — with our compliments.

What is love?

You may have gathered by now that the one thing we believe is the same about all people is that they're different. We are all unique, and have unique ways of thinking about things — about strategies, about success, and about love.

Historically and culturally, there have always been vast rifts in people's ideas about love. The Greeks had six words for it, none of which are quite the same as the way we use the term today. The aims of love have varied too. For many hundreds of years (and this is still true in many cultures), the only sane thing to do was to marry for money and the financial support a partner gave you; nowadays, taking a partner for any reason other than strong emotion has a variety of names, many of them unprintable. Even nowadays, in different cultures around the world, we find different ideas of love. So whereas Beela, a happily married Bengali woman, can serenely say that 'I did not love my husband for the first few years, but now I do', Debbie, a young English girl, will firmly state that 'I couldn't commit myself to any man I didn't love.'

If people have been brought up in the same culture and with the same background, will their ideas of love be the same? Not at all. In fact, consider your best mate — the one who lived opposite you, went to the same school as you, and played 'Who d'you fancy?' with you in the wine bar after work. Your experiences of life have been fairly similar, and when you have talked about relationships late at night over the second bottle of red, you've seemed to reach remarkable agreement. Even so, your ideas of love are probably very different indeed.

In broad terms they may seem the same, even though for you living together is fine whereas your mate seems to think marriage is a better deal. When it comes to specifics, you may consider rowing to be a prelude to the end of the world, whereas your friend may see it as the sign of a healthily developing relationship. And, whereas you might consider it a nice but unimportant gesture that your partner rings home when an hour late, your friend might see this as an essential sign of caring, without which the decree nisi is only a few inevitable steps away.

Another thing about love is that it seems to run in stages. You may have noticed this, even in a relationship that's going really well. The breathless anticipation of his phone call in week two has, by year two, turned to mild irritation if his phone call is an hour late. The total panic over the misunderstanding at the disco last night has resolved itself, four kids later, into a knowledge that if she isn't happy she'll tell you and you'll talk it through.

Many of the people we talked to spoke about their relationships as having stages. The first is that thunderstruck emotion that poets and pop songs refer to, 'jittery, with my head in the clouds. . .' (Liz), 'being totally focused on one person, all my thoughts and feelings. . . this is infatuation'. (Helen) And Helen's judgement was echoed by many people, who thought that feeling like you're high on champagne all the time is wonderful, but it isn't for ever, and maybe it isn't all that real anyway. It seems as if this very strong physical attraction is, at any rate in Western society, one of the main ways that we know we are *in love* with someone, but we are wary of it.

But later in the relationship, if it is to work, other factors take over — the issues that have to be resolved if you are to become an effective working partnership. 'Loving is more permanent' adds Helen, and Rose and Phil comment 'We work together and share everything equally.' For coming to terms with the reality of living with another person involves sorting out the practicalities, coping with tasks such as buying houses and rearing children. And two people trying to form an effective partnership also have to cope with differences of interest and opinion, pressures from outside, and the day-to-day challenges of meeting each other's needs when they may very well clash.

We did find evidence of people who were able to take their relationship even further. A hint here, a whisper there, of couples who had kept the total fascination with each other that was there at the beginning, had combined it with the effective working relationship that they'd developed over the years, and had added a third ingredient, an ability to rise above day-to-day irritations. No one did it completely, some people achieved it some of the time. We think it is the key factor in making love work, and we refer to it throughout the book in various ways, some obvious, some less so.

Ideas of love differ, and the stages of love differ, but one thing came through from everyone we talked to — the fact that being in a relationship is a very different experience. It can literally change the way you see things, and certainly changes the way you feel. As you read on through our account of how people experienced love, compare your own experiences. How do you feel, how do you think, what do you do when you love?

The main question we asked was 'How do you know you're in love?' and the first answers we got were almost always in terms of feelings, 'I know I love Terri because I feel bubbles inside' (John), 'I still get all fluttery inside when I know he's due home' (Rose). Loss of appetite, giddiness, breathlessness, stomach trembles, warm ripples... no, it's not the new mystery virus, but some of the common symptoms of love. It can be quick and sharp, a flash of emotion, or it can take over the whole body.

We noticed that no one claimed to feel good about their partner all the time; everyone we asked admitted to getting irritated or downright enraged on occasions. It seems too that many people become far more angry or upset with their partner than with ordinary friends or colleagues — maybe because they can be more vulnerable with lovers, maybe because strong negative feelings can go along with the positives. 'I only really get angry at people I'm close to; I can put up a front with anyone else' (Sue).

We discovered, by talking to people and by drawing on our own knowledge, that these feelings don't just come from nowhere, and it isn't a simple case of seeing your loved one in person and feeling strongly. We can feel the feelings even when our partner isn't there. How?

By using our heads. The pictures and sounds that we have inside our heads — our thoughts — take what we experience, make sense of it, and then suggest to us how to feel. Everyone does this differently, so there are as many wonderful varieties of thoughts, and as many wonderful varieties of loving, as there are people in the world.

> When I think of Frank, I see just his face, softly lit and in pastel shades. I hear his voice, low and soft. I always feel loving towards him when I think of him like that. (Eleanor)

In the language of the mind's eye, Eleanor sees Frank in a very particular way — and feels about him in a very particular way too. We found that many people thought about their loved one very differently from the way they thought about anyone else, not only in what they thought, but also in *how* they thought it — the *kind* of pictures or sounds.

> When I imagine Andy (a friend), I just see his head and shoulders. I see all of Maggie when I imagine her, and a much bigger picture. (Simon)

For our thoughts are built up by experience. We store experiences in our minds as a sort of identikit picture to remind us of people, and thoughts of the one we love are stored in a special way because we love them. As each meeting, phone call or other contact is made, this gets slotted in, to round out, and sometimes alter, our idea of our partner.

> If I think of Alan before we started going out, I see him as vague and indistinct. Now when I think of him as my lover, the pictures are bright and clear. (Tina)

The images don't have to be realistic — we found some that weren't.

> I see people as circles. When I feel close to them, the circles move together, but when I start to dislike them, the circles move further apart. Simon's circle overlaps with mine. (Maggie)

And very often, the way people knew they were in love was that they had mental images about the relationship in the future.

> I know I love Sue because I'm able to imagine us together in forty years and feel good about that. I've never been able to do that with a girlfriend before. (Ian)

One way I have been able to tell how much I love somebody is thinking about being without them in the future. The more I panic, the more I love them. (Sue)

These thoughts, as we said, are created by our experiences, and in turn, they create the feelings. The people we talked to about relationships that had ended said that once they had come to terms with the break-up, they thought about their ex-partner in a very different way. The content of the picture or sound may not have changed, but the way they saw it had.

I remember her as if she had rays of light coming from her, and saying my name in a particular loving way. I still sometimes think of her like that, but not so often now the relationship is going badly. (Shaun)

I know I'm ready to end a relationship when I stop asking myself whether my partner loves me and start asking myself whether I love my partner. (Lucy)

You may be beginning to realize that, if the thoughts create the feelings, then they are also responsible for a lot of what goes on in relationships — the things we do. Many a present has been purchased because of someone's clear picture of someone else's happy face. Many a conciliatory phone call has been made because of someone's memory of someone else's trembling voice. The person concerned wasn't there when the present was bought or the phone number dialled, but the memory itself, and the way it appeared, did its work.

At other times in the relationship, of course, that same language of the mind's eye can allow things to go very wrong. When a long series of bitter scenes have changed the close, soft-focus pictures to distant, dark, sharp ones, it can be difficult to summon up the enthusiasm to go home on Saturday night. When years of unmet needs have turned the soft, low voice into a loud, whiny one (in your mind, not in reality), it can be very easy to give it all up and head for a different person.

It seems, then, as if loving is about experiencing, thinking, feeling and doing. We meet someone. We experience their individuality. Our experience gets stored as thoughts about the person, and these thoughts lead to feelings. What we feel leads to what we do. Everyone handles all these things differently, everyone loves in a unique way.

In this book, we look at those experiences, those thoughts, those feelings and those actions. We see how other people handle them, and we allow you the opportunity to look at how you handle them. How do you think about your lover? How do those thoughts change as you experience her on a deeper level? How do those thoughts lead to your feelings, and how do your feelings create the way you behave, running the relationship in your own particular way? How does your partner handle all these things, and how does the way in which you both handle these things — the way you both love — influence the course of the relationship?

We'll suggest ways to make all these elements of your loving as successful as they possibly can be. We suggest ways to become more aware of what and how you are thinking, to refine the thought processes you have, and add new ways of thinking and responding. We show you how to become more aware of what you are feeling, to be more at ease, and to have more choice about how you express that emotion. We tell you new ways of doing things, new approaches to what you already do. And in particular, we suggest ways of allowing what you do and what your partner does to fit together more neatly, more effectively, more lovingly. In other words, we'll be giving you love strategies.

How do I use Love Strategies?
Having looked at what love strategies are, let's think about how to use them. You or you and your partner have some very special ways of interacting, problems that may be unique to you, certainly joys that no one else can ever dream of. So how can you take the strategies learned from other people and start really using them to take charge of your particular relationship?

One of the things that came over very clearly when we talked to people was that, even if they didn't realize it, they were using a set of skills to make love work. It wasn't only that they were feeling more emotion, or trying harder than anyone else; if anything, it was when they did things that were easy for them, and that they enjoyed doing. For you, like everyone else in or out of a relationship, are actually doing the best you can at any moment. So it's just a question of channelling your best in the right direction. Two tennis players will be putting just the same amount of energy and effort into a game, but the more skilful player will ultimately get the best results.

The other thing that came across clearly when we talked to successful couples was that they used the same skills whatever the issue. The same wonderful communication made shopping at the supermarket and negotiating over fidelity equally successful. Literally, it wasn't what they did, it was the way they did it. So the uniqueness of your relationship can slot very neatly into the processes we offer you, even though the content may be very different.

A third thing we noticed was that people who were successful in relationships were flexible. If they tried one thing to get what they wanted — to stop a row or create understanding — and that didn't work, they were willing to try something else. No one way of behaving, no one strategy will work consistently all the time. So if you try something we suggest, and it doesn't work — even if it worked last time — then try something else.

In the workshops we ran, we found the best way for people to begin to use the strategies was to work through the explorations. These help you to realize what questions other people ask, what issues they consider that make their relationships work, and then ask these questions for yourself.

> At the end of the first day of the workshop, we were asked to go home and write down a list of the things we thought were agreed between us. In the morning, we swapped notes. It was amazing to find out what Mark thought we'd agreed that I didn't know about, and vice versa. I never realized that we hadn't discussed this, or that other people did. (Lucy)

Doing the explorations also helps you use these strategies even after you've read this book and filled in the spaces!

> It seemed strange to write down exactly what I wanted from a relationship. I had to really convince myself that I had a right to ask for what I needed. When we discussed it in the group, I was relieved that others had similar wants to me. Since the workshop, I've mentally checked out before starting a new relationship whether it's what I want. I've turned down a few offers that I would have accepted before, but the ones I've accepted are a lot more satisfying. (Celia)

Doing the explorations with a willing partner may also be a very powerful experience for your relationship. To swap thoughts, feelings, needs and wants on a very deep level can open up whole areas of new ground, making it easier to communicate and to love each other more fully.

> When we did the exploration on telling each other how we needed to be treated when we were upset, I was amazed at how little I knew about Nicki's needs. I was almost in tears as she explained that what I'd been doing actually stirred things up for her more. Since then, she's been upset a few times, and knowing what to do makes me feel a lot more powerful and hopeful. (Rob)

Love strategies are about empowerment. Not power over someone else, but power over your own life and love. Knowledge is power, and knowledge about your own ability to love, and about your own love relationship, is the way to make things happen. Knowing just what to look for in a partner who will make you happy, knowing just how to make that partner happy, at a very detailed level, can totally transform your potential for good relationships.

So get curious about the way you work and the way your partner, prospective or actual, works. Become fascinated by what his movements, words and silences can tell you. Look out for how your needs and likes fit or clash. Notice ways in which you can make your partner feel good, motivate him, help him to understand. Just as if you were studying a complex piece of machinery to help it run better, look at the ways in which your relationship runs and could be tuned.

To begin, turn to Love Strategy 1.

2.

What are you bringing to the relationship?

When you begin a relationship, whether it's your first or the next in a series of many, you come to it carrying luggage. Your body, your mind and its skills, your personality and its glories. You come with your past memories, and hopes for the future. You come complete with your present situation, job, family, friends, other interests.

This Chapter looks at the way you can use the luggage you bring to enhance your relationship, and use your relationship to enhance the other parts of your life. For a relationship that demands that you abandon your luggage is a bit suspect, and luggage that is so heavy it stops you loving someone is very restricting!

Love Strategy 1 invites you to look at your situation and see in exactly what ways a relationship could slot into that. How can you choose a relationship that fits without letting your situation block you from the joys you could have from love?

To your present situation, you bring a past which defines the way you relate and the way you love. Love Strategy 2 looks at the messages from the past you carry with you, and how you can break free of the unhelpful ones.

In Love Strategy 3, we concentrate on you yourself, here and now. What amazing things do you have to offer to a potential partner? How are you different from anyone else, and what dangers and opportunities does this fact bring with it?

Whether you are already in a relationship or preparing your-self for one, this Chapter offers you a chance to step back and look at yourself before you start looking at your partner.

LOVE STRATEGY 1

Choosing a relationship that is right for you

People build their lives the way they like them. They choose flats and fill them with plants, take jobs and fill them with plans. They form networks of friends, relatives and colleagues and revel in being at the centre of the web. 'I have a cottage in Wales,' says Nicki, 'I go there every weekend, and I wouldn't give it up for anything.'

For anything, or only for a relationship? At first, love may seem a thing apart, but soon it may start becoming your whole existence. And what if you suddenly find yourself with a room full of car engine, or a house full of her friends, a job that is keeping you from your social life, or a social whirl that is severing your relationship with your family?

Successful lovers think it out beforehand. Some of the happiest and most satisfied people we met had looked at the different parts of their lives — homes, jobs, friends — given them a thorough spring-clean, decided what they could do without, and hung on to the rest. And *then* they chose a partner who was prepared to hang on with them, building the life that they wanted, within the restrictions that existed.

Julia and Joe got it right.

> I knew from the August onwards that I'd be moving abroad and that any long term commitment was out. It meant turning down two potential lovers, both of whom I thought would get too involved with me or vice versa. Then I met Gordon. He'd just ended a long relationship and was feeling vulnerable enough to want something quite short-term and uninvolved. I told him the very first night what my plans were, and we went out for eight months until I left. We're still friends. (Julia)

> When Andrea left me with the children to look after, I panicked a bit. After I'd recovered enough to think about settling down, I realized that it was a package deal — anyone who took me took the children as well, at least for the next few years. I was lucky meeting Katie; she liked the kids even though she didn't have any of her own. But it wouldn't have worked, however much I wanted her, if she hadn't wanted the children too. (Joe)

Could either of them have chosen otherwise? Of course. Julia could have unpacked her bags, Joe might have been able to offload the children. But once they had decided the situation they wanted, they stuck to that, and waited until they met someone who wanted that too. Gordon sighed with relief when Julia's short-term relationship needs met his, Katie adopted a family and began to discover the joys of having kids.

In fact, if you really get it right, the relationship adds to your situation, and your partner's. A new partner can often mean a whole new social life, more resources, or someone to cat-sit while you're away.

> We did fancy each other, right from the beginning, and the relationship has always worked well. But we have to admit that being together has also allowed us to buy a house, which neither of us could have afforded alone. (Caroline and Pete)

Think of it as an ecological issue. In some ways, like the alpine flowers or jungle orchids, we are dependent on our context, our surroundings, our situation. We've built this up for ourselves, chosen the flat, the job, the mates, the hobby to be as appropriate for us as veldt is for the gazelle. Change the surroundings, alter the balance, and you have an unecological situation — for you, for your partner, and for the happy-ever-afters.

The love strategy used by the people we talked to was simply to know what they wanted, which bits of their own particular landscape they were prepared to change, and which had to stay the same in order for them to survive. They gave their partner an accurate map and together they developed an environment that was ecological for both of them.

So how can you use all this? You can begin with the following exploration, a life map which helps you plot your own life situation and find out where a relationship would (or does) fit in. It's something we use at the start of workshops to get people thinking about their situation.

If you're between relationships or at the breathless start of one, this will help you get things in perspective. If you have a partnership, take a look at the way it helps (or hinders) your life. Your partner may want to do the exploration too, so that afterwards you can talk through your discoveries together.

The diagram (see page 30) shows the various areas that might be part of your life. These are our ideas — add or subtract any that you need to, and move the areas around if you want so that they reflect your own situation. Reading through the notes we've made on each, jot down your situation, then ask yourself the questions we're asking.

Work

Whether it's a paid nine to five or the more than full-time job of parenting, work takes up most of our time. So how important is it to you? Would you willingly give up your job tomorrow if Ms or Mr Right came along — or would your partner need to realize that your job is part of your self-esteem and identity? 'I'm an actress' says Celia 'and almost anything I do needs to come second to my work.'

What job-related problems would a partner have to cope with, or maybe help with? We're workaholics, and know that very few people could put up with the 1 a.m. finishing times we set ourselves. Together, though, we can keep ourselves going when the fourteenth cup of coffee has failed to take effect.

If a full-time job is not the way you spend your day, 1 a.m. deadlines may not be an issue. But money may be, and a partner who felt that dinner at the Ritz — with you paying your way — was an ideal way to spend alternate evenings, might prove to be more trouble than he's worth.

Living situation

Where do you live? Far from the madding crowd — or just far from your maddening lover? When George and Anna met on a singles holiday in Corfu, they rather liked meeting only at weekends once they got back home; it allowed them time and freedom in between. Paul and Liz stuck weekend commuting for a year before moving in together to stop them drifting apart. So think about just how far away, when it comes to relationships, is too far for you.

'I couldn't bear to actually live with Chris' says Pete, 'we'd drive each other up the wall.' If you have a real need for personal space, it's fairer on a partner, and on yourself, to admit it before he turns up with suitcase and toothbrush on the second date. If there are other restrictions you need to work within, such as hostel rules or suspicious landladies, take account of these too when briefing a prospective lover.

How could a partner offer home improvements? Tina loved

acting as amateur interior designer for Alan's newly bought house. Trevor moved in with Eve as a temporary lodger, stayed as permanent lover and both of them benefited from improved living conditions. It's never a good idea to take a partner simply to gain a flat, but if it comes as a free gift, why not welcome it?

Free time
Two minutes before bed, or every evening and the whole week-end? Make a note of what free time you have, and a note to choose a partner with a compatible leisure pattern.

And what do you do for leisure and pleasure? If you're firmly committed to freefall parachuting, however much you may want a partner to share the experience with you, this may take some negotiating! John and Terri, after many partners who had not found their interest in vegetarianism and massage appealing, found that they did appeal to each other. 'When I realized that Terri was aware of diet, I knew that our lifestyles wouldn't clash.'

Maybe, though, there's room for a new interest in your life and a partner's fresh viewpoint on free time. Because of Ian's interest in bicycles, Sue has just, at 36, learned to ride, skinned knees and all.

People
If your idea of ecstasy is to be a hermit for months on end, you may not have many people in your life. Most people, though, are surprised by how many there are when they jot down a list of all their friends and acquaintances, family and relatives.

But how important are all these people? Your Sunday after-noons (or your days and nights, for that matter) may be spent caring for aged Uncle Albert, or having quiet pub lunches with a series of ex-lovers with whom you have relationships that are almost but not quite platonic. A new lover needs to work within this.

So be aware of your people patterns, which you want and which can go. A new lover may give you the chance to give unwanted friends the push, and pull your social situation into shape. They can give you a whole stream of new people to see, and let you view your old friends with new eyes.

Now you've mapped out your world, where are you? How would a partner fit, in terms of time, space, commitment? What restrictions would they have to navigate, with your help, to make the relationship ecological for both of you?

On the other hand, what are the selling points of your particular line in lifestyles? Not the delights you yourself have to offer — that's covered in Love Strategy 3 — but the joys of your having sunny summer days readily available, a tribe of helpful friends, or a time-share on a villa in Lanzarote. Someone somewhere who has what you want would slide into your situation as neatly as the last piece fits into a jigsaw puzzle.

Equally, what could you get from having an equal partner around? 'What I needed was someone who could understand my real commitment to the job,' says Dave, a youth worker on a training scheme. 'Within a month of meeting, Mary had got involved. Our honeymoon was spent taking the kids climbing in the Lake District.'

Love Strategy 1 is about fitting round pegs into circular holes. What all the people in this strategy have shown us is that our particular lifestyle and our particular love style can add to, not subtract from, each other. If we really want to, of course, we can redefine our priorities, abandon everything and follow our beloved to the Alaskan wastes. But given a little forward planning and a heavy dose of pragmatism, we can also find a partner whose needs meet our own, and who can delight in taking advantage of what may seem to us like our disadvantages.

Fig. 1 LOVE STRATEGY 1

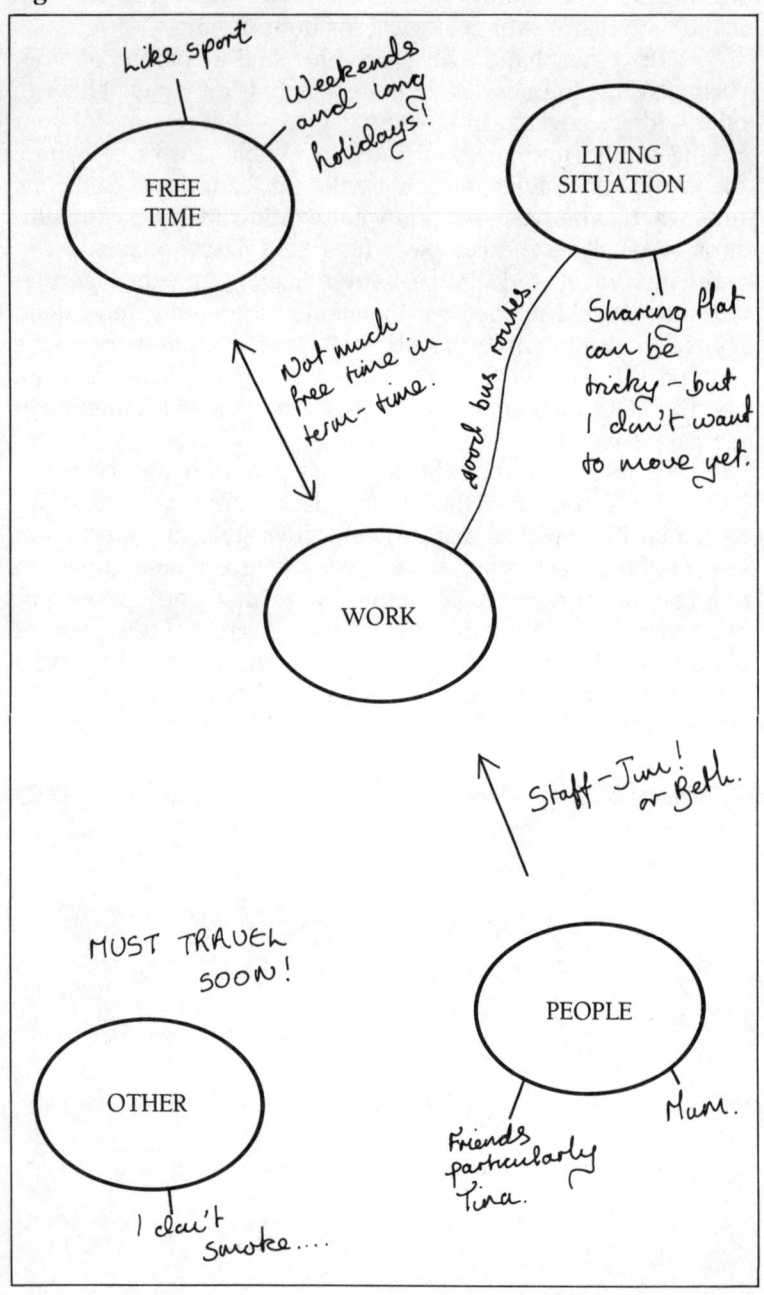

Fig. 2 LOVE STRATEGY 1

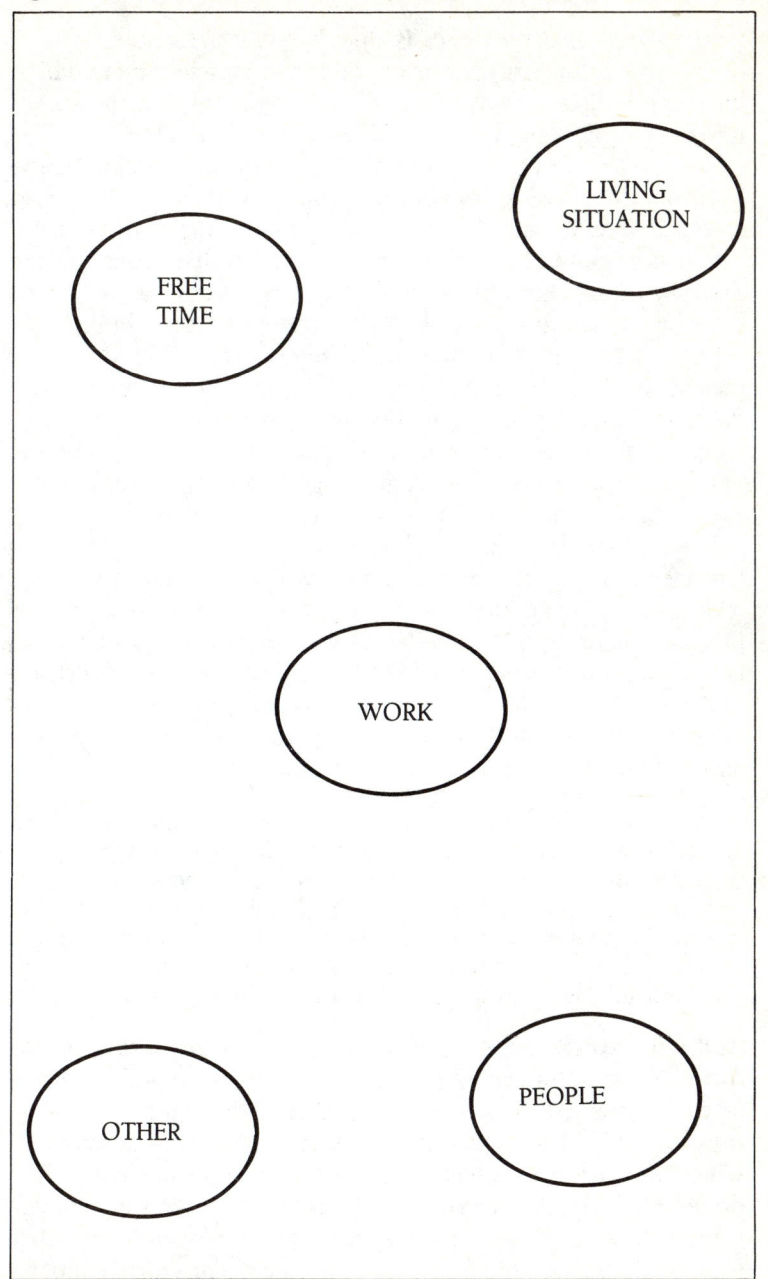

LOVE STRATEGY 2

Cutting free of a past that is affecting the present

If we told you that in your head you have a movie camera which has been whirring away from the very moment that the sperm joined the egg, would you consider us totally mad?

Well, in a way you have, and we dispute the claims of insanity! For from the very start of your life, you have been able to record in some way, feeling, hearing, seeing everything that went on. The boom boom of Mum's heart, the smell of disinfectant in the delivery room, through to your first fuzzy sight of your Dad or your brothers and sisters — it's all in there. In your brain.

More than that, it's there for a reason. The first time you picked up something sharp or tried to grab the flames in the fireplace, it hurt; and the movie camera whirred away, and you recorded a memory not to do that again. But when you reached out for a nipple and got sweet-tasting good stuff, or smiled and got a hug, the message was — yes, do this again.

People, people, people, all around you; as a child, as a teenager, as an adult. And the camera whirring, not only on your own direct experiences when a big boy hits you in the playground, or your Mum tells you you're great. The camera also keeps going when your best friend gets kissed behind the cricket pavilion — or raped behind the disco — and you learn from that, almost as much as from your own experiences, to relate, to hate, and to love.

> We both realized when we met each other how much we'd been influenced by our home lives. I think that was what helped us understand the problems we had. Rose has memories of her Dad never congratulating her on her school reports — so if I didn't say nice things about her, she got really upset. I was brought up in a divorced family, and reacted in all sorts of ways — unable to give, unable to trust. I learned all I know about love from Rose. (Phil)

And what you learn, even if it's a shadow or distortion of 'the truth', is what you keep hold of. When you see something nasty in the woodshed at eight, you shudder at the sight of a pile of firewood at 18. Rose's misery at home turned into a vulnerability when her husband behaved the same way that her father had done. Similarly, Phil learned not to trust his parents and found himself thinking Rose untrustworthy too. It can work the other way of course — 'Boys are nice to kiss' can turn, step by enjoyable step into 'Sex is wonderful' — but the mechanism is the same. We keep the tapes stored, and when we see or hear something similar, we drag out the old film with a cry of recognition.

The film analogy is actually quite realistic. Most people do think by making pictures and sounds inside their heads. These may be selected cuttings from real events in the past, or ones imagined from things they have heard or read about. A glimpse of sister kissing boyfriend good night, a snippet of disillusioned conversation overheard at work, and the whole movie changes, along with the feelings we have about it.

The feelings change because coded into each picture and sound are the messages we received about the feelings involved. You will have your own personal coding system, but it's more than likely to involve, for example, close, soft-focus pictures and low, slow voice tones for people you feel romantic about. If experience teaches you that this is not someone to feel romantic about because she went off with your best friend, then the focus of the stored picture might sharpen up and the voice might suddenly become higher and faster.

> I'd had quite a lot of bad relationships in the past. When I met John, we didn't sleep together for weeks because I kept remembering other people and getting dark, gloomy pictures of the future. In the end, I had to literally look at John and tell myself he was different. The pictures seemed to brighten up, and I knew that it wasn't going to be the same this time round. (Terri)

Terri, like Phil and Rose, used Love Strategy 2. They all became aware of what in their past was affecting their ability to love in the present. Terri had learnt from several lovers (rather than two parents) that relationships were unhappy and were always going to be like that. She felt it so deeply that she coded it in to her pictures of the future. When John came along and reminded her of other lovers by being a potential lover himself, up came the pictures, coded for gloom. It wasn't until Terri realized that John was different that she felt differently, and in response her pictures literally brightened up.

All three of these people, once they had realized what was happening, were able to switch off the film, turn off the tape recorder, let go of the old script. This isn't then. This is now. They did it in a number of ways, knowing that the success of their relationships depended on it.

Identifying the messages

So how can you do this too? What strategy do you need? Switching off the film is the second step. The first is realizing that it's running, realizing which messages you've got in your head, and then deciding whether you want them there.

The exploration is in two parts. On the left, there is space to write a list of people who might have passed messages on to you, about yourself, your possible partners, or about love. Once you've read through the list and identified key people in your life, allow your mind to go back to times you were with them. Do any pictures or words come to mind? Any messages from the movie, on love and how to do it? There may only be one or two messages, 'Married people always row!', 'Sex solves everything!'. But they will be there. Write them down as you go in the middle column.

As a rule, messages come from people, but there are other rules than that. Rule number one is that the more people, the stronger the messages. One friend crying after a failed relationship is sad. Two is not a coincidence. The chances are that after six consecutive broken-hearted companions, you're likely to have learnt some pretty unerasable lessons concerning the pitfalls of falling in love.

Rule number two is that the earlier the people, the stronger the messages. Mothers and fathers are the most likely unknowing message-bringers, as they struggle to keep their own relationship going with all their own mental messages going full pelt as well. So young people learn that older people who are in 'love' are liable to support and care for each other — or to get angry and unhappy.

It can work for you. Eleanor and Frank both reacted strongly against oppressively tidy parents, and got messages in their minds about real love being the freedom to leave things where you will. They now live in a four-storey house with attic where every room is piled high with their belongings — and they're blissfully happy.

As well as mothers and fathers, there are a whole tribe of other relatives ready and waiting to influence you without knowing it. And the closer you are to them, the closer in they can get. Jane's sister went to her first grown-up party and was kissed unwillingly. 'She didn't seem to mind, but every time I imagined it, I felt sick. I still can't bear to be kissed.' When the present reminds her of the past message, up come the pictures, these ones coded for nausea.

Culture, too, can be shocked as well as shocking. If all around you, family, friends, school teachers, and religious elders believe that partnership should be planned by proxy, not passion, you are likely to feel, as Beela does, that 'Respect between husband and wife is more important than love. Love causes problems.' And as a result, you may (or may not) be happier than Karen, who loses her virginity at 16 because her cultural norms give her the message that that is expected. And, if all around you, the media is proclaiming the glory of page three, you may well be forgiven for getting confused between those two four-letter words, love and lust.

Friends, and especially young friends, may well be your worst enemies when it comes to messages. Friends can spend many a happy hour discussing 'him' or 'her' — the glance he gave you at the bus stop, the chance word in the school corridor that keeps you going for a week. But you are all in the same position, often surrounded by self-doubt and ignorance, and many an adult hang-up has first begun by an adolescent friend piling bad advice on bad. 'You can't get pregnant if you do it standing up'; 'If you're jealous, that means you love her.'

Yet some of the best, wisest and most loving messages we heard in the course of writing this book seemed to come from friends who had, when people were unhappy, reassured them of their self-worth with that knowledge that can only come from long years of knowing the worst as well as the best. 'I spent two hours talking through the whole thing with him, and in the end he just looked at me, no spiel of advice, and said, "You can do it." I could have hugged him.'

When you start your own relationships, that's when all the hearsay becomes reality. Four things can happen. Your opinion of yourself can go up or down. Or your opinion of your love partners can go up or down. A series of kind and genuine lovers telling you that you are good in bed will raise your spirits and literally brighten up your self-image; while the opposite can mean a lifelong message of failure for both sexes, and possible impotence for men. Misunderstandings, mismatches and good old mistakes can alter your whole trust in other people, while a series of positive experiences can give you a clear belief that lovers are loving and partners never drift apart.

Sorting out what you want

Once you have got some answers about your own pattern of messages, you can start asking questions. We have left space for you to write in any interesting answers you discover. Which messages of thirty years ago are still dictating what you do today? Which beliefs of today have you never questioned because they came from someone thirty years older than you whose opinion you valued? Which events of today just take you straight back to the original message, with all the accompanying feelings you had as a six-year-old, even though at 46 you can actually cope a whole lot better now?

And the bottom line. Which messages do you still want around? Find the ones that make you feel good about yourself, that make you stand up straighter, walk taller, and feel more aware of your own potential to love, and of the potential of love itself. Explore them, find out more about them, making your memory and your self-esteem more solid.

Then track down the ones that undermine you, make you cynical or powerless, unrealistic about your partner's limitations and strengths. You may not want them, but they may keep coming back. Old films tend to crop up again and again, and not only on rainy Sunday afternoons on the other channel. You may already know very well what you're doing when you confuse your lover with your father and feel the same feelings you felt as a child. So what can you do to erase the tapes?

Perhaps one of the simplest ways is just to step out of them. Seeing what happened to you back then can change your point of view. If you hear a message you don't want, try playing it backwards a few times; next time you hear it forwards, it may feel different. It's difficult to feel the same about a film when the projector's broken.

Another way to break unhelpful links with the past is to pour a strong dose of the present over them. Could your partner help by pointing out when you're confusing her with a past lover? Could you help your partner by reminding him that just because his schoolmates said he was fat doesn't mean that you think he is overweight? Talking about the message and where it came from has the same effect in relationships as rattling crisp packets does in the cinema — it suddenly makes the film very unreal.

So, armed with knowledge of what's going on, try to choose the film you want to watch, the one that gives you and your partner the pictures and the words to make it a happy, loving ending.

Fig. 3 LOVE STRATEGY 2. Exploration

| PEOPLE | MESSAGES | | HOW DO THEY AFFECT ME |
	PICTURES	WORDS	
EXAMPLE PARENT Mum.	Hugging me when I was bad.	'Love the person, not the action.'	Very tolerant of my partner.
PARENTS			
OTHER RELATIVES			
SCHOOL			
BOOKS PLAYS...			

Fig. 4 LOVE STRATEGY 2.

	PEOPLE	MESSAGES		HOW DO THEY AFFECT ME?
		PICTURES	WORDS	
RELIGION CULTURAL BACKGROUND				
FRIENDS				
PAST RELATIONSHIPS				
PRESENT RELATIONSHIPS				

LOVE STRATEGY 3

Capitalizing on your uniqueness

Imagine yourself as a rather rare and almost extinct species of very beautiful animal, a sort of bipedal, slim-line version of the Giant Panda. For, given seventy years or so, the sad fact is that you will be extinct. The happy fact is that you are more than rather rare; you are totally unique. Given cloning, the genetic engineers may come pretty close, but they will never be able to reproduce the exact experiences that have made you uniquely you.

So take a closer look at this custom-built special. There will be times, of course, when you find it hard to believe that uniqueness equals quality. What's the point, you may ask yourself, in having a paunch to be proud of, or being, without any shadow of a doubt, the worst conversationalist in the world?

The point of that is that you're missing the point. Worst and best are only comparative anyway. In some cultures, the aforementioned paunch would be a sign of affluence and achievement. Redefine worst conversationalist in situations such as a tricky negotiation, where keeping your mouth shut and listening is a carefully refined and valued skill, and you begin to see that whatever you've got, you've got going for you.

> I was fairly convinced, at 26, that I was totally unpair-off-able. Everything I did seemed to be at odds with what everyone else was doing, and I couldn't imagine anyone else fancying me, so I kept myself very much to myself. Then one day, when I was talking to Mary, my landlady whom I'd known for ages, I made a comment about being odd, and she looked at me amazed and said 'You mean you're a one-off?'. Well, I thought, that's a new way of looking at it. We started going out the following week! (Dave)

Dave managed to realize that best and worst, like sexy or friendly, are only the labels people (and you) put on you. If you peel off the label saying eccentric, and replace it with a big bright sticker proclaiming 'genius', things start looking different. Love Strategy 3 — capitalize on your uniqueness.

You do have to have the sticker, though — in your own head if nowhere else. People will believe you if you say you can't cook, and they will believe you if you act that way, as they sit back replete after the cordon bleu five-course meal you've just cooked them. But if you see yourself as valid, then others will value you, and if the price tag says millions, that's what people will pay; in hugs and compliments if not in cash.

Find out your strengths

So how to get the celebratory sticker? We've provided you with your own, a full page of space to fill in your strengths and assets. We suggest you take some time over this exploration. If a voice in your head tells you that you have nothing to offer and that the sideboard needs dusting, remember that the polishing effect on your life and self-esteem will be infinitely more valuable than the polishing effect on the mahogany.

If necessary, call in the support troops. Who can tell you, in genuine tones, exactly why they like being with you? Your best friend from school, your children, or the work colleague who's always appreciated your showing him how to use the new word processor? Using our ideas as starting points, get others to point out your strengths.

Your body
What's beautiful about it, what's healthy and in good running order?

Your mind
What insights, thrills and nice surprises does it give you?

Your emotions
What are the feelings that delight and move you?

Your achievements
What are you proud of in your life?

Your skills
How skilful are you — with people, with tools, with words?

Once you've assembled a list of all your assets, you may well be feeling good about your uniqueness. 'I feel best when I'm with the kids,' says Barbara. 'I know that I am the only one that they've got, and no one else could literally take my place.'

You too are a one-off. In fact, your whole world is totally unlike anyone else's. You are unique because you see your world through different eyes and hear it through different ears from your friend, your boss, your lover.

The experiences of childhood make us each interpret what

happens in a unique way. We look and listen for different things. We remember different things. Very early on, we find ourselves regarding different things as important or irrelevant.

Watch infants let loose in a playground. Watch who heads for the swings, the roundabouts, the other children. At four, they already have their priorities, their loves, things they ignore, things they are afraid of. Now watch adults let loose at a party. Watch who heads for the food, the drink. Listen in to the conversations and hear how past experience has also made each one see the world in a totally unique way.

'Well, you always lose friends when you divorce' means that he does. 'Money is the only thing to consider in a partner' means for her. 'We don't sleep together any more; we're too old for that' means in their opinion.

To get to know a little bit more about the unique way that you see the world, try doing this exploration. Get together with a friend or partner and talk about an experience you both have in common. Tape it, then listen to the tape afterwards. When you really start getting fascinated, you will discover that there are certain patterns to what you are saying, about the things you notice and the things that are important to you, about the pictures in your head. In particular, notice what words you use to describe what's going on inside you — do you see 'dark futures' or feel 'bubbly inside'? What are your particular patterns?

How are you different?

Notice too how you are different from other people. When you listen to the taped conversation, you will notice how the things that you mention are very different from the things your friend mentions. And next time you're with other people, listen to what they are saying, and then listen to yourself. You will soon spot the differences between their world and yours, between what's important to you and what's important to them. It could be that the same things are relevant or irrelevant to you. Or it could be that you're literally worlds apart.

This may seem scary. Whereas people who are or have what we want can be fascinating, people who experience the world differently from us can be threatening. But they need not be if you remember that this is a sign of their uniqueness and a reminder of yours.

Yes, Kim is very different from me. She loves making lists of things to do, planning our lives out weeks in advance. It makes her feel secure. I work the other way, living from day to day. I suppose this could have been a problem, but we realized very early on that it was just because we were different. I like Kim's lists, and she values my spontaneity. (Paul)

Paul had a strong enough sense of his — and Kim's — own uniqueness not to feel threatened by the fact that they were different. He used Love Strategy 3 to see things in a new way, and celebrated when their world views were different.

We are all different because we each develop like an exotic, rare animal, in response to our surroundings. The gazelle's long legs help it survive by running, while the whale's blubber has developed as a protection against the cold. The boss's avoidance tactics may have in the past helped her to avoid death by overwork, and your lover's hard shell may be a result of protecting himself against childhood rejection. Everyone's camouflage is there for the best possible reasons — survival as a unique person.

This very uniqueness can make you increasingly valuable. You have things no one else can offer, and you can fit a partner's needs in a way no one else in the world can. For couples are made from two sets of uniquenesses. When Sue's unique ability to organize met Ian's unique ability to generate an endless stream of new ideas, we ended up with a series of projects which kept us both in work. When Jan's bounce met Malcolm's stability, they produced a happy family life for their two daughters.

So revel in your own rarity value. Like the Giant Panda, you are in short supply, and anyone who gets you can be thankful. Use that confidence to go for the things you value in others. Capitalize on your uniqueness to find someone as unique as yourself!

Fig. 5 LOVE STRATEGY 3 Exploration 1

Fig. 6 LOVE STRATEGY 3

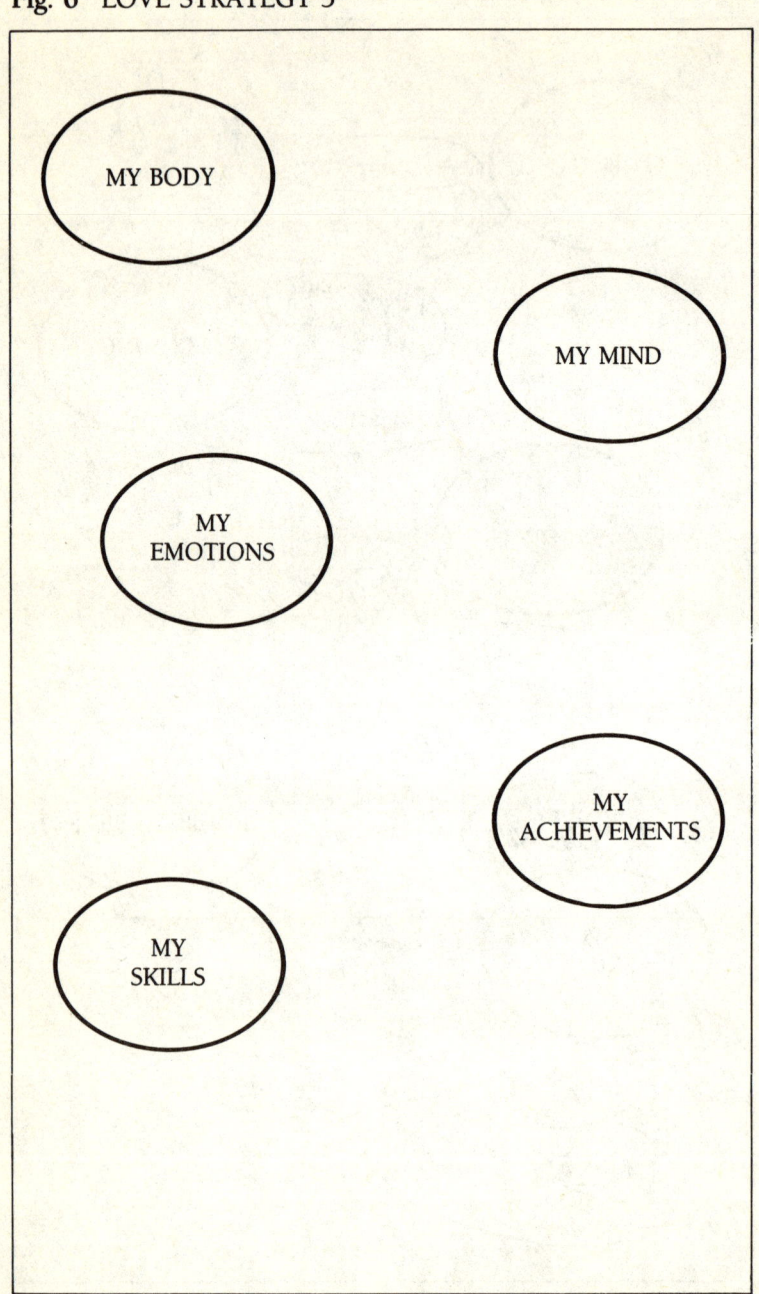

LOVE STRATEGY 3
Exploration 2

1. What are you talking about?

2. Are you more interested in
   (a) what there was (things)   ☐
   (b) what's happening (activities)   ☐
   (c) who was there (people)   ☐
   (d) where it was (place)   ☐
   (e) when it was (time)   ☐

3. Are you more interested in yourself or in other people?

4. Do you notice what is good or what is bad about a situation?

5. Which do you notice more, how people relate or what was achieved?

6. Which do you notice more, who or what is there in a situation, or who or what is missing?

7. Which do you notice more, the similarities in things, people, situations, or the differences?

8. When you talk, do you concentrate on collecting information for its own sake, the ideas or principles involved, or just for what's useful for the future?

9. You will probably have been talking mostly about the past, because you were talking about a memory. But in general, which interests you most — the past, the present or the future?

10. When you talk, what words do you use to describe your 'language of the mind's eye'? Do you refer to pictures in your head, saying things to yourself, or emotions that you feel in your body?

3.

What do you want from a relationship?

This Chapter is about wanting. As we shall see, the word want can be an unacceptable one, and wanting love can be even more unacceptable.

Love Strategy 4 is about finding out what it is like for you when you do want or don't want, and rediscovering the ways you have of finding out what is right for you and what is wrong. It also indicates some areas to look at when deciding what you do want from a relationship or a partner.

Once decided, it's important not to compromise, but to choose a partner who has what you want — and also one who really wants you. Love Strategy 5 points out some of the problems involved in doing this, and some of the ways of resolving them. The main thing is — have the relationships you want, and don't have the relationships you don't want.

LOVE STRATEGY 4

Knowing what you want
Have you lost the gentle art of wanting? You had it once, maybe longer ago than you can remember. Small children have no sense of self-denial. An embryo responds unhesitatingly towards a source of pleasure, and a baby never stops to worry about who else might want its mother's milk. Very young children are amazing absorbers of good things, from sunshine to smiles, and avoiders of bad things, from cross voices to sharp objects. When it comes to deciding what they want and what they don't want, they have no need to stop and think. They know.

As they grow older, the messages start to come in from outside, and slide into their minds and bodies. 'I don't care what

you want' hears the screaming two-year-old. 'Never mind if it
tastes bad, eat it' hears the stubborn four-year-old. At five, you
learn not to take the last cake on the plate, and you also learn to
confuse the signals of need from inside. As a method of getting
along in a world full of other people, it's necessary and effective.
As a way of keeping in touch with what's right for you, it leaves a
lot to be desired.

By the time you are ready to leave your parents' partnership
and start your own, you may well have lost the art of really
knowing what is good for you. You may have forgotten that
subtle interplay of body feeling and mental images that tells you
that doing this, feeling that, agreeing with this person or going
out with that one are the right things for you at this time in this
place. Like a spider in the centre of a web of sensations and
emotions, you could be delicately sensitive to what is going on
around you, saying 'no' or 'yes' easily and without guilt. So often,
however, this is not how things are.

The same applies to choosing a relationship. Do you know
what sort of partner you want? You may think that it seems
hard-hearted to consider your own needs when you should be
concentrating on meeting the other person's requirements. And
in any case, if you flourish your shopping list of wants too
obviously, you'll scare people off, won't you?

In fact, we all choose all the time, whether we are aware of it or
not. How much better to have worked out exactly what you
want before making a choice, than to be guided by what other
people think. In the long-term, knowing just what you want can
be a far more loving way to start a relationship. If the tables are
turned, which would you prefer, a partner who knew what they
wanted and knew it was you, or one who wasn't quite sure and
was using you as a way to find out?

Listen to your body
How do you find out what you want? For Tina, it meant listening
to what her body was telling her.

> I didn't know what I wanted for a long time. I'd been going out with
> Stuart for about six months, but somehow I wasn't happy. I was
> tired and constantly seemed to be ill, with vomiting and diarrhoea.
> In the end, I realized it was the relationship that was wrong for me,
> not anything to do with what I was eating. (Tina)

Most people don't get as strong a reaction to a wrong situation as Tina did. But the world reaches your mind through your body, and that is where you will get most information about what's happening and whether it is right for you.

Think back to a time when something you did was right for you. Whether it was a room well decorated or a business contract clinched, your body will have joined in the celebration briefly, with a sigh of relief, a tingle of excitement. It may only have lasted a second, but it will have been there. 'I think of what I want, and then just feel "that's it"; a sort of nod, all down my body', says Maggie. Equally, if you go ahead with something that is wrong for you, your body will signal that too. A sudden tension in your stomach, an unaccountable feeling of tiredness at the thought of what there is to do. Warning bells and red lights for you to take notice of.

So often, though, we don't take notice. We block off our awareness of what is happening, inside and out, overriding the signals with messages about selflessness, duty or needing to get the job done. You may find, if that happens, that the signals fade away as if anaesthetized out of existence. If the problem is serious and you simply won't listen, however, your body will continue to sound louder and louder warning bells, with sleeplessness, distraction or, as in Tina's case, nausea.

If all else fails, your mind may take action on its own account to stop you doing things that it feels you shouldn't. If you consistently sabotage a situation it may be because your subconscious knows that it would be disastrous for you to succeed. 'I knew something was up, but I didn't know what,' says Ric 'I kept trying to get a steady relationship going, and failing. Then I realized that in fact I really wanted to do some travelling first, before I could even consider settling down.'

The opposite, of course, is that total body feeling that accompanies the certain knowledge that here and now, this person is the right one to be with. The euphoria, the energy, the feeling of total immortality that accompanies falling in love; or the easy, relaxed contentment of a partnership heading towards its twentieth happy year. These are your body's way of telling you that you are getting what you want.

Reading the messages
You may well listen to your body's signals, but be unsure about

what they mean. You seem to be following the path you want, hand in hand with the person you want, but something is wrong. What is it that you really need in order to feel good? The same blocks to body feeling, erected by time and other people's messages, may stop you from becoming aware of the exact content of your desires.

But the pictures in your head and the things you say to yourself may well be able to give you more information. The people we talked to had some wonderful mental ways of finding out what was best for them. When Katie wasn't sure about sleeping with Joe, she literally saw in her mind a picture of a brick wall, which was blocking her from committing herself sexually. When she got to a point where she could trust Joe, the picture actually changed so that she could see beyond the wall and see him waiting for her beyond her fears.

Frank knew Eleanor as a friend for two years before he realized that he wanted a more serious relationship with her.

> I was at a dance. I hadn't gone with her, but she was there, sitting across the dance floor from me with some friends. All evening, I felt uneasy, and I couldn't put my finger on why. In the end, I literally heard a voice in my head saying 'Because she's over there, not over here' and I realized that what I needed was Eleanor. (Frank)

If you are unsure what is best, then, allow your mind to give you more information. Literally stop, look and listen, not to what is happening outside, but to the pictures and sounds inside. They may know more than you do about what you want.

Look at what you want in a partner that is different from your own qualities, and what you want that is similar. Difference, it seems, is the one that strikes first, that often forms the stomach-churning attraction of initial contact. 'Ian was just so self-sufficient' says Sue 'and I compared my sense of vulnerability and dependence, and thought "I want access to that".'

'Having access' is a phrase that was echoed in one way or another throughout many of the conversations we had. Alex, relaxed and unemotional, wanted access to Lyn's bouncy enthusiasm. Eve's intuition wanted access to Trevor's logical love of information. For many people, there seems to be a pull towards others who will complement, provide strength where there is seen to be personal weakness, or supplement where there seems to be need.

Difference and similarity

In the more long-term sense, however, many couples need a large overlap of similarity in order to co-exist. Particularly where people move to share day-to-day living patterns, contentment is found where lifestyles, opinions and goals are fairly similar. Eleanor and Frank admitted that 'We both love youth hostelling and the ballet. We're both librarians. We're both exquisitely untidy. We can understand each other.' In everyday life, from first mortgage to retirement plans, partners need to move through the world in the same direction.

As we shall see in later love strategies, this delicate balance between difference and similarity can be what makes or breaks a relationship once the first excitement has faded. Too similar and you get bored. Too opposite and you get homicidal. The message is; when you look at what you want, look at the balance.

Equally, when you look at what you want, be specific. The words we use to describe love are gloriously vague; 'romance, devotion, commitment, fidelity'. But what do they actually mean? More importantly, what do they mean for different people — particularly for you and your lover?

> When we met, Ian said he needed to be 'mothered' occasionally. I wasn't too sure whether 'mothering' was my strong point, but was very happy to give it a try... When depression next struck, I zoomed round with hot meals and did the ironing, only to meet with blank amazement. What I had meant by 'mothering' was physical nurturing. What Ian actually needed was his version of the word — lots of emotional permission not to be in charge all the time. (Sue)

Again, those video cameras inside our head give us each totally unique recordings of what we mean by any word. For someone with Ian's background and experiences, mothering meant being allowed to be vulnerable; for Sue, it meant tea and sympathy.

We get lulled by everything around us — by our friends, our parents, our television, our romantic novel or our girlie magazine — into believing that of course we know what love is. And in fact, its smallest expression can be totally different for each of us. 'You don't love me' mutters Joanna, as she drags herself to bed wearily after another row, thinking wistfully of shared massages, restaurant meals and afternoon delight. 'No —

it's you who don't love me,' claims David, as he mulls resentfully over the fact that all Joanna wants to do is relax, never really to work on their relationship by hammering things out. They're both right, of course — and they're both wrong.

Beware of simplifying
Wrong, too — or rather, dangerous — is the temptation to simplify, to believe that as long as our partner gives us the main thing we need, then all our needs will be met. Sex, intellectual stimulation, a shoulder to cry on — all these are wonderful, particularly when celibacy or a previous partner meant denial of these needs for so long. But if we concentrate only on one main need, we are liable to find the others are ignored, or that we have confused one need for the other. Liz looked for security after an insecure first marriage. After a series of men had offered security through dominating her, she finally realized that she also wanted comfort and support, and was able to give up partners who physically abused her.

Equally, if one overriding need drives us into a relationship, once that need is fully met or we have grown beyond it, the relationship may no longer be relevant. The first unsuitable affair solely in order to lose one's virginity, the confidence building exercise after a broken marriage, the work relationship which springs up as an afterthought to overtime — all these can develop to meet one need, and may wither as soon as the need dies.

The exploration
The exploration we offer you for this strategy is based on something two of our interviewees actually did. We now use it in our workshops, to get people focussing on what they do want.

> We'd both had disappointments, and were both fed up with not getting our real needs met. Coincidentally both of us had written down a list of what we wanted from a relationship; mine was part of my New Year's resolution list. I wanted someone who shared my interests, who could communicate with me, who was interested in diet and massage. When we met and were attracted, we shared lists. They were remarkably similar. (John)

The fact that John wrote down what he wanted didn't conjure Terri up out of thin air. Nor did it guarantee love at first sight or a permanently rosy future. But it did make him aware of what he actually wanted from a relationship; so when Terri happened along, he was able to recognize immediately that she fitted his needs, and this made him far more able to welcome her as a partner.

We have adapted John and Terri's basic strategy to form a checklist of issues you might like to consider when working out your wants. If you have a partner, you can compare notes, though this may be more appropriate when you're tackling Love Strategy 5, which is about choosing a partner who has what you want and wants what you have. Concentrate for the moment only on what you want for you.

For each issue we've suggested, decide just what you want. Get back to that basic ability to feel whether it is important or not. Would it matter for you if it wasn't part of your relationship? Which issues have we missed out that are vital for you? And are there any things you want that needn't necessarily be supplied by your partner but could happily be fulfilled by friends?

When you have completed your list, choose half a dozen of the most important things on it, the ones without which you wouldn't consider a relationship to be a success. Then sort out your priorities. If companionship is more important than sex, for example, you'd want a very different relationship from someone who put them the other way round.

Once you've got your priorities right, go back through the list again. For each want you've chosen, decide specifically how you would want to experience it in real life. What would you be doing if you got what you wanted? What would your partner be doing? Think in real unambiguous terms. If *support* means doing the washing-up, say so. For your partner, it might mean talking into the night, or paying your way through college.

The exploration will almost certainly get you more in touch with what you really want. It needn't end there, of course. Given the chance, that beginning can allow you to reclaim the gentle art of wanting from where it got lost early in your childhood. You can start to feel what it is like being satisfied with what is happening around you, with what you are getting, with how you are being treated.

And you can begin to sense the signals telling you that no, this is not all right; that demand, this objection, those people are actually wrong for you. Slowly, gently, without a four-year-old

temper tantrum and without a 14-year-old sense of
unworthiness, you may soon be able, as spontaneously as the
four-month-old you once were, to move away from what is bad
for you and towards what is good.

LOVE STRATEGY 4
Exploration

What I want in a partner

In the present

Physical qualities
What would your *ideal* partner look like?

What physical qualities (e.g. age, strength) are particularly
important?

What physical qualities would actually prevent you going out
with someone?

Mental qualities
Rank these qualities in order of importance to you:
   practicality
   intelligence
   creativity
   organization
What other mental qualities are particularly important to you?

Achievements
Everyone achieves some things. But in what area would you want your partner to be an achiever (e.g. work, study, sport)? Are there any achievements that are particularly important to you?

Attitudes
Is it important to you e.g. for your partner to hold certain attitudes about any one thing (e.g. politics, religion)? If it is important, which attitudes do you need him/her to hold?

Approach to life
What sort of person to you need your partner to be (e.g. bouncy, quiet, sensitive, someone who gets things going)?

Interests
How important is it to you that your partner shares your interests? If it is important, which kind of interests do you enjoy, and therefore want your partner to share?

Social interests
How far and in what ways do you need your partner to fit into your social scene?

How far and in what ways do you need your partner to bring you into his/her social scene?

Sexuality
Do you need your partner to have particular sexual interests (e.g. heterosexual, lesbian)?

What is the ideal attitude to sex for your partner (e.g. celibate, tender, dominant)?

For the future

Goals
Which of these goals do you need your partner to have and which would you definitely be against him/her having?
Fame, fortune, power, great achievements, a family, quiet life, just plain fun.

The far future
How far into the future should your partner think (e.g. a week, a year, a lifetime, a millenium)?

Should your partner dream of great things or consider only what's practical?

Your partner's wants and needs
What must your partner want in a relationship?

What other aspects of a partner are important to you?

What I want in a relationship

Time commitment
How much time would you want to spend with a partner (e.g. one evening a week, every day)?

Space commitment
In what ways would you want or not want to share space with your partner (e.g. live together, not allow your partner to visit your home)?

Resources commitment
In what ways would you want or not want to share resources with your partner (e.g. income share, let him drive the car)?

Sexual commitment
What sexual commitment would you want from your partner, and what sexual commitment would you want to give?

Social commitment
What sort of commitment of free time and activities would you
want from your partner, and what would you want to give (e.g.
see friends separately, play sport together)?

Formal commitment
Ultimately, what types of formal commitment would you want
the relationship to be heading for (e.g. marriage, children, living
together)?

What other aspects of a relationship are important to you?

LOVE STRATEGY 5

Choosing a partner who has what you want and wants what you have

Think of a relationship as one of those delicately carved Chinese
puzzles. When all the bits almost fit but not quite, it can hold
together or fall apart. When all the bits do fit, it's amazing.

People can be like Chinese puzzles. You have needs and
wants, strengths and weaknesses. So does everyone around you,

the milkman, your Mum, your children — and your partners, present or prospective. If you choose someone who has the pieces that you need, and who needs the pieces you have to offer, you have the basis for a relationship that will give you everything you want for as long as you want it. If only a few pieces fit, and those loosely, you may be on the road to disappointment — or to a good life-long compromise.

If you know what you want, there will be certain things that are essential — what sex your partner is, for example, or what age. Some people can be wonderfully flexible about this, but for others the dividing line between acceptable and unacceptable is narrower. You may laugh at the lonely hearts ads which specify that applicants should be between '32 and 44' but to take a partner thirty years older or younger than yourself is still unusual, and courageous.

On the next level down, what's important? Physical appearance often is. People who would not dream of walking into a car showroom and saying 'I'll have that one because it's red' can still be found walking into a disco and saying 'I'll have that one because it's blond.' Then there's the issue of common background. Does he come from the same town as you, did she go to the same kind of school? What course are you studying, what job are you doing, how long ago was the divorce? All of these questions reveal if the person opposite you on the dance floor will be your total opposite when you stop dancing.

On a still deeper level, consider personality. Do you want stability, or an ability to have fun? Support, or a willingness not to pry? Your own needs, your wants, the messages in your head will all tell you what sort of person you need. 'I wanted someone relaxed and confident' says Lyn 'I looked across the room, and there was Alex.'

Meeting that someone who seems to fit your particular shape of puzzle can be the most wonderful experience in the world. Your whole body responds to tell you that this is right, and that you should follow that person doggedly round the world for the next forty years. Tina felt this, very strongly.

> He came to see my flatmate, and I stayed to chat. After we'd talked for about two hours, I knew he was what I wanted. He was going out with someone else at the time, but I stayed friends with him for a year, because I knew he had everything that was important to me. In the end, we started going out, and eventually we married. (Tina)

Tina used Love Strategy 5 — to go for someone who has what you want because you are likely to be happy with him.

Tina was lucky, though. For her, the pieces fitted exactly (although, as we learn later, for her partner the fit was not so snug). For many of us, a newly-met partner may meet many of our requirements, but not all of them. How many, for you, is enough?

At 16, willingness is often sufficient. Anyone who will value you enough to spend Saturday evening in your company may have everything you want or hope for. At 26 or 46, the expectations — and the value you place on yourself — are higher. Even so, needs vary, and what is more than sufficient grounds for marriage with one person may be grounds for divorce with another.

'My husband respects me, and he has a good job. He is kind to the children. I am very lucky' says Beela. 'I'm a difficult person to live with' says Ric, 'I need someone who is prepared to travel, give me loads of attention — and be on their own even at weekends.'

Find your minimum requirements
So what is the bottom line for you? How much or how little would someone have to do for you in order for the relationship to be worth the bother? It's an interesting exploration, finding out what your minimum requirements are, and one that can allow you to take a different view of things when storms are brewing. Remember, though, that if someone doesn't have what you want, you have a choice. You can remind yourself what you've got going for you and then go and find someone more to your liking, or you can work on improving the potential of the relationship.

Remember, too, not to expect a partnership to give you everything you want. The Chinese puzzle is made up of many pieces and only the largest is your partner. It's unfair to shoehorn someone into fulfilling needs they can't fulfil. Either don't form a partnership with them, or let the other things you need in life come to you through relatives, friends, people at work, or your own ability to go out and take what you want.

Of course, relationships are about giving as well as taking. And there's no point in choosing a partner you want if that partner doesn't need you. There is a certain, bitter-sweet masochistic pleasure in pining after someone who doesn't essentially value you for yourself, but, like acne, with luck you grow out of it. Of course, 'being valued' is a subjective phrase anyway, and whereas you may not consider yourself as valued if your partner sleeps with other people, your best mate may place far greater importance on whether her partner consults her over the finances.

Desire and rejection

Wanting what you have and having what you want in a partnership leads to several possible permutations of desire and rejection. All but one of them seem doomed to disappointment, but equally, all of them can be reversed.

The first possibility is that neither of you want the other. At first glance, this may seem like the ultimate dead-end; but at least one of the couples we interviewed actually began this way.

> We hated each other at first sight. It was quite funny really. We were both in the same play, and we used to really upstage each other and wind each other up. Then at the last night party, we started to talk, and found we actually had a lot in common. We've been going out ever since. (Lucy)

A lot of seeming incompatibility can be due to context. In the context of work, Lucy and Mark fought like cat and dog. But their interests and aims were the same, and when they weren't competing, they got on well. The Chinese puzzle fitted — but only when it was moved to a different shelf. Not all couples are so lucky, but then if there really is no fit on either side, there is little sense of loss, either.

A sense of loss usually occurs when one or others of you wants, and the other doesn't. If you have ever been the object of someone's attention when you see nothing attention-grabbing about that person, you will know the sad and yet defensive feeling of being pursued. 'He just kept hanging around all the time' remembers Dave, 'In the end, I told him straight out — and then worried for week afterwards about what I'd done.'

It would have been more of a worry if Dave had not been honest. If you really feel guilty about turning someone down, then think long and hard. Is there any way, given time, that this person might fit your needs? If not, then be direct. When you know that you don't want someone, either in the short or the long term, saying 'yes' at all can only prolong the agony for them as well as for you.

There is far more agony for you, though, if you are the one doing the wanting. Can anyone truly understand the horror of needing someone who doesn't care, if they haven't been through it themselves? Of watching, stomach churning, as she chats to her boyfriend, or he swoops off on yet another men-only club weekend?

It is possible to change things. The floating factors in this situation are yourself, or the other person. But a word of warning here. It is never really possible to alter someone else's opinion of you unless deep down they want it to be altered. Equally, if you try to be someone you're not, sooner or later — maybe after fifteen years of strained marriage — the real you will pop up and demand its birthright.

But people can change their minds. At first, the man Tina thought was the right one for her saw her as the wrong one for him.

> At first, I just saw her as a friend. As far as I was concerned, she wasn't what I needed at that time. She didn't have my background and I felt she didn't fit into my lifestyle. Then I began to see things differently. I realized that what Tina herself could give me, as a companion and a lover, was more important than how she fitted into my image of what a wife should be. (Alan)

At first, Alan didn't consider Tina to have what he wanted, and as long as this was true, he followed Love Strategy 5 and didn't start a relationship with her. Then he changed his mind, and his priorities. When he began to see Tina as meeting his needs, they married.

Alan spontaneously changed his point of view. James, on the other hand, changed Helen's mind for her.

> I actually didn't want a boyfriend at that time. I was far too into my job, and saw a relationship as a drag on my energy. But James was really interested in supporting me in my career, and convinced me that I could have both him and my job. (Helen)

The key, if you want to try persuading a partner that what he really needs is you, is to find out what is important to him. If you can meet that need — for career support, fun, stability — without compromising yourself, you may find that his desire for you mysteriously increases. If you can find out what she fears she will lose through having a relationship — a good social life, the chance to travel, her virginity — and happily give her a relationship that keeps those things intact, then you may find that her objections mysteriously evaporate.

The ultimate example of Love Strategy 5 has to be the system of arranged marriages. What couples who enter successful arranged marriages want may be very different from what couples from other cultures aim for. But the important factor is that partners are chosen specifically to meet each other's needs, in a way that 'romantic' partners rarely are. 'There is a culture-wide agreement about what is important in a marriage' says Beela. And unless individuals have wants and needs outside these cultural parameters, then partners probably do meet each other's needs.

Finding how your partner fits
To find out how closely your partner, potential or actual, fits with the Chinese puzzle that is you, try this exploration. Make a list of things that are important to you in a partnership. You may have got some ideas about this from Love Strategy 4, or you may like to think of some new ones. Choose the vital bits, the ones that friends or relatives can't fulfil for you.

Then think about how far your partner, or someone you would like to be your partner, fits the bill. Be aware of when things are right or wrong because they feel that way. That uncomfortable feeling of mismatching when you even begin to think of the girl in the next office as a potential partner is your body's way of telling you that this is not what you need. The relaxed 'that's it' as you realize that your boyfriend is the one you want is the signal that you've chosen well.

It may be that the person you've longed for just isn't the one who would make you happy. You may find that the person you always wanted and the person you are actually with are in fact one and the same. Or you may find that the ideal in your head is not the one you make coffee for every morning.

If you have a partner, get him to complete the exploration too and check his list against yours. If you can listen to each other's wants, where you fit and where you don't, you can gain an enormous amount of knowledge. Armed with this knowledge,

Fig. 7 LOVE STRATEGY 5 Exploration

THINGS IMPORTANT TO ME IN A PARTNERSHIP	DOES MY PARTNER MEET THIS NEED
Motivation to get out of myself.	YES!

you have a far better chance of ultimately fitting together as a pair.

Even if your partner appears to come with a pure-bred pedigree and meet all your needs, things — and people — can change. As we shall see in later love strategies, you or they can develop into a totally different person. 'At 20, I wanted someone to look after me and bolster my self-confidence,' says Tricia of her first husband. 'At 30, he hadn't changed, but I had. I found him dominating and a prig.' 'I watched my last lover take the job, and get more and more involved, and suddenly leave me behind. I had no place in his life any more' says Hugh. And so partners and partnerships drift inexorably apart.

Here, though, we are talking about choosing, not about making things work. And there is no reason, given adequate awareness of what you want, why you shouldn't make a good choice. Avoiding the temptation to settle for a best that is considerably less than second, you can size up the pieces, sort out the concaves and the convexes, slide them into place, and make a match. It may take some time, and some careful planning, but your Chinese puzzle may well have a solution.

4.

How do you get close?

Once you're in a relationship, the first months are about getting close — close enough to make each other happy, to support each other. Also, if a long-term relationship is what you want, close enough to begin to trust each other and move through the realization that the ideal you were attracted to is not the reality.

Perhaps the bedrock of any relationship is being able to communicate with your partner. Love Strategy 6 is about clear communication, not only by listening and talking, but also by seeing and being seen and feeling emotion. How can you make all communication positive and effective?

Much of the attraction you feel for your partner at first may be because you recognize a kindred spirit. But being close is about working with difference too. Recognizing and acknowledging your own and your partner's uniqueness, and using that as a basis for meeting needs, is the subject of Love Strategy 7.

But sometimes, particularly when past history gets in the way, it's hard to feel close. Differences can dismay, and even minor things can create bad feeling. Love Strategy 8 explains why bad feeling can arise, and offers some ways of dealing with it.

The skills in this chapter are relevant in any part of a relationship, from the beginning onwards. Use them to found, develop and consolidate your partnership, and to end it if that is the right thing to do.

LOVE STRATEGY 6

Getting clear communication
At its best, communicating with your partner is a dance. You move together, responding each to each, and aware of the

slightest movement in the other. Late at night and the wine all gone, or drowsy early morning conversations; good feelings all round, and the deep knowledge that you understand and are understood.

The dance of clear communication is essential to moving through your relationship successfully. For while many of the relationships we looked at used only one or two love strategies, we didn't find a single relationship where the partners didn't communicate in a way that pleased them both. 'I don't know what I'd do if I couldn't talk to Caroline' says Pete. 'Leave her, I think.'

What is this clear, clean communication that is so necessary? It seems to be about thoughts, and about feelings. When one partner talks and the other listens, and the experience of the first is recreated in the thoughts of the second, that is communication. When both are left feeling good, even though they may disagree on the topic, that is successful communication.

So what stops the dance? What makes us stumble and trip against each other, unable to move together? One answer seems to be lack of awareness, a simple failure to notice, to gather information about what is happening for your partner, and for yourself. This can stop us really understanding what is going on for the other, and start us spiralling into a mudbath of unpleasant feelings, simply because we don't notice what's happening until it's too late.

> Very early on, we tried to learn each other's signals. Both Rob and I have a very complex set of cues — the way we move, a special tone of voice — that can signal to the other one that we are in a particular mood, or have particular problems at that time. It took a while to learn what meant what — but now I know when he needs to be left alone, or when he really needs to talk. (Nicki)

Nicki and Rob looked and listened, and started to pick up the hidden messages beyond what was actually being said. So often the words are the tip of the iceberg, of euphoria, of depression, of insecurity. The way someone comes through the door, the way they say 'yes' or 'no'; all these can let you see what's underneath, and allow you to understand the real meaning behind the surface conversation.

Looking and listening

Where to look, and how to listen? Perhaps one of the first things to do is learn to be quiet. If you are one of those people who hears what someone else is saying while rehearsing your own lines for the next part of the conversation, try this. Next time your partner is talking, turn down the volume of your own voice in your head and just listen. You may well find yourself noticing things she does and says that you have never been aware of before. How does she express her feelings? What is her repertoire of signals?

Don't bother comparing with someone else; even if your ex-husband's smile meant anger, your lover's smile may mean joy. Notice instead when your partner's laugh seems strained — and when you notice that same laugh coming again, realize it's a valuable signal.

One exploration we offer people at workshops is to look and listen to their partners and check out what is happening. If you haven't yet found a partner, you can do this with a friend — perhaps even one you want to be even more friendly with.

Notice what you can see and hear when the other person is happy, angry, sad and so on, and jot down your observations on the grid under these headings.

Quickies

These are the sudden, tiny movements that you need to watch or listen carefully for. Examples are: a sudden intake of breath; a tiny nod or shake of the head that tells you when someone is going to say 'yes' or 'no' long before they say it; a catch in the voice; a blush; a sudden tensing of the shoulders, chest, stomach.

Eyes and face

Most of the signals we pick up from each other in everyday life are from the face. Examples are: eyes changing shape; eyes looking up or being 'downcast'; pupil-size changing (a subtle one, this); smiling; frowning; mouth movements such as a grimace.

Posture

You can often tell what someone is feeling when he's across the street just by the way he carries himself. Examples are: slumping; breathing slowly and low in the chest; 'walking tall';

breathing high and quickly; curling up in a chair or on a cushion.

Voice
Even over the phone, you can work out the state your loved one is in, by listening to the way he's speaking. Examples are: slow, low tones; fast, high, quick speech; trembling voice; particular emphasis on words.

> I can always tell when Sue's not too sure of something; she gets a far-away look in her eyes and goes very still. Then she squints very slightly, first one eye then the other, as if she's literally weighing something up in her mind! When she's come to a decision she looks straight at me again and starts talking. (Ian)

Awareness of your partner. Awareness of yourself. They're both as important as each other, but you may need a mirror to tell you just how you look and sound! In fact, it's much more effective to do the exploration, and get your partner or friend to tell you how you come across to them.

Don't worry about the tiny things, the tightening of the mouth when you're concentrating, the change of colour as you get worried. In the heat of a heated moment, you won't notice those anyway. But if you become aware of how you always play with your hair when you're feeling tired, or begin to hear that particular pitch your voice takes on when you start to get irritated — that's useful. That sort of awareness can spot a war approaching a mile away, and stop it in its tracks!

Internal signals
Much more subtle than voice pitch, and even more effective in peace-making, can be increasing your awareness of what's happening for you inside. As you've read this book, you may have begun to become sensitive to the internal feelings that we call emotions. Happiness may be a tingle down the spine, anger a tension in the shoulders — and love is all sorts of nice (and sometimes nasty) feelings almost everywhere. Being aware of them can double your control over what is happening. If your partner becomes more aware of his feelings too, you can quadruple it!

> When we're talking, I'm often not aware of my body at all. Then if John says something that seems threatening for me, I feel a

churning in my stomach. I know that now, and know that if we don't stop and do something else, get close, or resolve the issue, very soon I'll get angry. (Terri)

Terri has got to know her own body signals, and when they come, she knows it is time to take action, or have a row. You may choose to row (many couples do), but if you want clear communication, then a row is not the place. So use the first twinge of uneasiness as a danger signal to take avoiding action. Hugs, smiles, cups of tea, any comments that will draw both your attention to the way feelings are heating up, all these are good cease-fire tactics; for others, turn to Love Strategy 8.

Mixed messages

Sometimes, though, it's not as easy as spotting tension in your partner or frustration in yourself, because 'mixed feelings' can be just that — a mixture of emotions or thoughts that drag you this way or that. 'I'm in two minds' you say, wondering whether to go to that party or not. 'On the one hand I feel . . . but on the other hand . . .' mutters your partner, uneasy at the thought of a holiday apart. Be aware of mixtures of feelings, excitement and anxiety mingled, a desire to be honest clashing with a fear of rejection. Watch out for contradictions between what is said and what is seen; the relaxed expression as she tells you the bad news that she can't see you tonight because of overwork. Or, perhaps the worst of all double signals — the eye contact sliding away as your partner responds to your words with a hesitant 'And I love you too.'

Such mixed messages are confusing both for you and for your partner. If you feel two feelings, it can be difficult to work out which is the real one. If you notice your partner feeling two feelings, you can well become insecure. For who is at ease when faced with a partner who doesn't know what he wants?

The answer to this type of message is to admit that you are in two minds. An admission that you aren't sure will short-circuit your own fear, and your partner's fear of what you are feeling. A straightforward statement from the other person that he doesn't know what to do will be something you can cope with, where mixed messages may leave you gibbering in a corner. 'If I say straight out that I feel bad,' says Maria 'rather than worrying what Ric will think of me, he can understand that.'

Asking and telling

Awareness does not have to be a matter of subtle cues or small signals. As well as watching or listening, you can ask and tell. To really allow your partner into your world, to let him experience things as you experience them, is one of the most effective ways of communicating, and of getting close to one another.

I often ask 'What are you thinking?' and Ian will tell me the thoughts that have been running through his head. We exchange ideas like that all the time. Sometimes he will literally describe his thoughts by telling me how he sees things or hears things in his mind. I'm always amazed at how different he is from me, although sometimes we're quite similar too. (Sue)

If you want a really practical demonstration of clear communication, try this exploration that we use in workshops. Get together with your partner or a close friend. Start talking about a particular incident that you both experienced — an evening out you spent together or a meeting you both attended.

Then listen as your partner lets you into her world. Perhaps a world of activities where yours is of people, or a world of sound where yours focuses on sights. If you are close enough to ask more deeply, then ask what's going on inside her head. Let her tell you more about her representations — the colour, the focus, the clarity, the speed. A memory that is dim and shadowy for her may shine and sparkle for you; or she clearly remembers certain conversations while you can't even remember what you said yourself. Then ask what her feelings are, compare notes on past memories or future hopes, and end up amazed at how deep communication can get.

The exploration questions from Love Strategy 3 are repeated here to help you concentrate on some of the things that it may be useful to you to notice. What exactly is your partner talking about — things, people, activities, places or times? Is she interested in information — or how it will be useful to her? And just what sort of things does she experience in her mind's eye? 'I see a long uphill struggle ahead' may tell you a lot about her world and the pictures she is making in her head.

A further exploration is this. Think of a film you've seen but your partner hasn't. Use your new knowledge of her, her likes and dislikes, the way she experiences the world inside her head, to tell her about it in a way that really interests and enthuses her.

If your interest is in activities, but your partner's is in people, tell her about the last thriller you saw (activities), but stress the characters in it (people). If what makes your partner feel good is bright, sparkling colours, then concentrate on that crowd scene in the snow-covered Alps, not the dim night-club scene that appealed to you. Then swap; can your partner tell you about a film she has seen in a way that enthuses you? The advanced version, when you're ready for it, is to use the same new knowledge about your partner to help her understand something you have been trying to explain to her for a long time.

If your aim is to dance together, even if the beat gets tricky, then you will do it. Whoever is following and whoever is leading, whoever sets the pace and whoever keeps the rhythm, it takes two to tango. And if you both keep looking and listening, aiming for communication and sticking with honesty, you'll probably win the Dance Championship — as well as the Nobel Peace Prize.

Fig. 8 LOVE STRATEGY 6 Exploration 1

	QUICKIE	EYES/FACE	POSTURE	VOICE
EXAMPLE SURPRISE	Sudden intake of breath	Wide eyes	Sits up.	Voice goes up.
HAPPY				
ANGRY				
SAD				
SUDDEN THOUGHT				
WORKING SOMETHING OUT				
GOING TO SAY 'YES'				
GOING TO SAY 'NO'				

Fig. 9 LOVE STRATEGY 6

	QUICKIE	EYES/FACE	POSTURE	VOICE
LIKE IT				
DON'T LIKE IT				
REMEMBERING				
TOTALLY SURE				
UNSURE				
UNSURE AND TRYING TO HIDE IT				
EMBARRASSED				
TURNED ON				

LOVE STRATEGY 6
Exploration 2

1. What is your partner talking about?

2. Is he more interested in
    (a) what there was (things)
    (b) what's happening (activities)
    (c) who was there (people)
    (d) where it was (place)
    (e) when it was (time)

3. Is she more interested in herself or in other people?

4. Does he notice what is good or what is bad about a situation?

5. Which does she notice more, how people relate or what was achieved?

6. Which does he notice more, who or what is there in a situation, or who or what is missing?

7. Which does she notice more, the similarities between things, people, situations, or the differences?

8. When he talks, does he concentrate on collecting information for its own sake, the ideas or principles involved, or just for what's useful for the future?

9. Your partner has probably been talking mostly about the past, because she was talking about a memory. But in general, which interests her most — the past, the present or the future?

10. When he talks, what words does he use to describe his 'language of the mind's eye'? Does he refer to pictures in his head, saying things to himself, or emotions that he feels in his body?

LOVE STRATEGY 7

Getting close

When eyes meet and you suddenly realize how precious this new person is, the thing you are most aware of is how similar you are; how you like the same things; how your new world is right just for the two of you. Closeness is as natural as breathing.

Later, even just a few hours or days later, getting close seems a bit more uneasy. The discovery that he doesn't like your kind of music, the unfamiliarity of a new body in bed, the realization that she is far tidier than you are. The emotion, often the passion, carries you through, but there are distances. Like explorers discovering a new world, it's scary once the first excitement is over.

The way to get close is actually to enjoy how far apart you are. Once you've measured the distance and become aware of the ways in which you are each unique and different from each other, you can start to bridge the differences by appreciating them. This is Love Strategy 7.

The first thing to remember is that, like the pieces of the Chinese puzzle we talked about earlier, it's often the differences themselves that make the fit. It seems that we are first attracted by those we see as complementary. When shy meets confident, relaxed meets bubbly, careful meets carefree, we feel we have met our match. But the other person's complementary attitudes also bring with them basic differences in outlook or world view that you may find distancing. If so, try realizing that without the differences, you might not have the compatibility.

I was totally drawn to Liz's strengths, the way she thought clearly and logically, the 'groundedness' she felt. It seemed to offer me something that my emotion and energy couldn't yet provide. When her world view starts to get on my nerves, because it seems too cold and unemotional, too unresponsive to the world, I have to remember that this is part of the package. (Kathy)

For your partner, like you, is a one-off, and however much the sharp edges may rub you up the wrong way, that's the shape she is.

Sharing your worlds

If you are willing to find out what shape your partner is, where she is metaphorically concave and convex in the way her mind and her emotions interact with the world, you can get very close to her indeed. First, you can understand the way she works, and delight in it. Also, if the way she works is not the way you operate, you can be amazed by it. And, if it does not threaten or compromise you, you can meet her particular needs. You can almost shape your world to meet the shape of hers, and fit snugly and compatibly into it.

One way of beginning to explore your partner's special topology is to remember that you are a late arrival in her life. Even if you have known her since childhood, and are her first ever lover, other things will have happened to her which have made her what she is. To really understand this, read Love Strategy 3, and if you already have, let us remind you that we are all the product of past events, past messages, past people. Your partner has a stack of videos in her head that would keep a film festival going for a century — and they have created her, her ideas of love and her reactions to you.

Many of the people we talked to found that, particularly in the early days of a relationship, exploring the past and these messages was vital to understanding and getting close to a partner.

The catch phrase for Rob's previous relationship was 'there's a time and a place for everything'. We talked this through a lot, and it wasn't until I understood what had happened to create that catch phrase that I could begin to understand why he reacted to sex the way he did. (Nicki)

It's a wonderful, binding experience to be able to talk about the past up to the time you met. Like sharing secrets as children, you can whisper under the bedclothes all the things you never told anyone, your innermost thoughts and feelings as you grew up in the world. You can share and learn just how your partner's parents thought of marriage, just what her big sister told her about sex, how he lost his virginity, how she came to have the abortion — and listening and caring, you can also learn how to care more, by taking all these experiences into account.

You can do more than just listen. It is in the love situation that we can best create or recreate the most powerful love experience most of us have ever known — being cared for by parents. Some of us will remember sadly childhoods where love was lacking. Some of us will recall happy times with supportive parents. Being with your partner is the time to recover or newly create all this.

> We often play. We can get so childlike, lying back to be cuddled, feeding each other or bathing each other. It's wonderful to be little and cared for. I feel that to be able to stop being grown-up, just for a while, helps me to cope with the outside world better. (Hugh)

Specifically, though, what remains in the present of what has happened in the past? Certainly past events affect what you think and believe, your expectations about the ways of the world on which you base your whole way of life. At first in a relationship, these expectations may not be apparent. They're not standard conversation fare at the disco, and even after a while it may come as a surprise to find that your partner has totally different views from your own — and just as unshakeable ones. Does he really believe that holidays in the sun drain his energy? Can she honestly think that she is overweight? That relationships should be worked at? That rows are constructive? That living together will restrict her freedom?

Appreciating the differences

The thing to remember, as you vary from delighted amazement to a feeling that this person was brought up on another planet, is that he is an alien being. His world is not your world. He is sitting there feeling just as alienated from you because of your ideas and expectations as you are from him because of his. The very realization of that can often cut down the distance between you to merely an arm's length.

One of the by-products of your partner's ideas about the world is that different things will be important to him. If he believes that a truly fulfilled partnership involves having a family, then children will probably be important to him. If she believes that her parents' marriage failed because of infidelity, then the chances are that to her, honesty and faithfulness are important qualities in a partner. So you may find that what are total irrelevancies to you are the focus of life for your lover — and vice versa.

> Until I met Maria, Mexico was just a place on a map. Through going out with her, I learned a lot about it because it was her birth place, and I developed my interest because it was important to her. When we went over for the wedding, I really got involved, and since then my whole view of the place has changed; I get very excited now by the thought of going back, and have begun to like all sorts of things Mexican. (Ric)

It could be that what is important to your partner holds no appeal for you. If the thought of going hang-gliding or attending the family Christmas party makes you feel nauseous, then that's a signal that it is not right for you. But so often someone else's compulsions can become compulsive for us too, and add a whole new dimension to our lives. One of the best ways of getting close to someone is to love what they love — be that a hobby, a career, a friend — or a vision of changing the world.

If you are not compelled, but not repelled, by someone else's focus of attention, look around for ways that it could be interesting to you. You don't have to go pony trekking all summer, but an occasional weekend could bring you closer to your partner and be an enjoyable experience in itself. When Sue decided to do ballet again after a three-year break, Ian came along to a one-off beginner's class, and happily pranced around too, just to see what it was like. 'Because it was a one-off, I didn't feel I had to go back, and Sue felt supported just by my being there. And it was good fun.'

For Ian, fun is important. He was able to go to a ballet class (important to Sue) because he saw it as fun (important to him). This principle can spread throughout your relationship, as you join in your partner's compulsions not because you're desperately trying to please, but because you have found something in his compulsion that appeals to you too. Your partner may go to the party because he likes dancing. For you, talking to the people there may make it all worthwhile. 'Caroline works late because she enjoys it, and she hates to miss deadlines' says Pete 'I stay up helping because it seems a romantic thing to do — and because I love to see her happy face when I do.'

Different things in life are compelling for different people. As with Caroline and Pete, what motivates you may not motivate your partner. Other things about the way you respond to the world may differ too. The way you understand things may leave him confused. The way you dream about the future may not get her enthusiastic at all. The way she feels unhappy or ecstatic may not mean anything to you. Think how it could affect your relationship if you knew these important things about your partner and could use them to make the relationship run more smoothly.

Day-to-day awareness

Important things can bring you closer, and so can small things. If you just notice the way your partner experiences the world on a day-to-day level, you'll probably be aware of differences right away. Gazing over a sunlit river, you may immediately be aware of the birds, the landscape, the sound of the water — while your partner is waxing lyrical about the construction of the oil tanker slowly moving downstream.

Knowing what your partner will notice can help you get close. If what he notices is people, then tell him about the people in your office, not how you struggled all day with the word processor. On the other hand, if machines are a focal point, the word processor may be a good conversation starter. If your partner always notices what is good in a situation, try making her happy by happily describing the good things about your day. On the other hand, 'I can usually rivet Kim to the chair by telling her about the problems I've had' says Paul 'Because what she notices in life is problems'.

Because your world is uniquely yours, not everything in it is going to be riveting to your partner. If you know this, you can not only choose to share with him the things you know will interest him, but you can also realize that his lack of interest does not mean a lack of love. And both of these will mean more closeness.

Now think about thoughts. We've already considered how minds work, popping up pictures, sounds and feelings to inform our bodies and process our ruminations. Yours are a special product of your past and your present. So are your partner's. And it probably comes as no surprise that when the way you see the world in your head is different from the way she listens to the world in hers, the distance between you can seem enormous.

Past experiences may mean that in her head, loud sounds mean excitement. so her idea of a really great evening may mean a night-club, while yours is a quiet restaurant. Happiness for you may be a bounce in your stomach; for your partner it may be a voice in her ear telling her she's happy. Our internal experiences are gloriously different, and can mean that we often don't understand the way each other's minds work. What can you do?

> When we first moved in together, bright colours literally made Maggie feel ill. I liked primary colours, and had a lot of red and blue cushions in my bed-sit. I couldn't understand why Maggie was getting so defensive whenever I mentioned bringing my cushions along. We realized that when she thinks of someone she's angry or upset with, she sees them in her head in bright colours. So to have bright colours around her makes her feel bad, and very threatened. Once we'd recognized that Maggie wasn't just being awkward, the whole thing was easier to handle, and we planned the flat to take into account both our needs. (Simon)

Taking into account everyone's needs can mean looking at how we see, hear and feel things. Maggie and Simon had problems about how things look; other couples found that voice tones or mattress thicknesses were a problem.

Touching — the way you like giving and receiving touch — is another area where differences can cause distance. If a hard touch is threatening for your partner and reassuring for you, admitting that may help considerably. If because of past messages, your partner doesn't like being touched in certain places, or certain situations, then you need to recognize that this is not a rejection of you.

We teach people in our workshops to be able to get and receive the sort of touch that is right for them. Taking it in turns, they 'coach' their partner to hug them in just the way they want, hard or soft, tight or loose, long or short. Do you like a bear-hug, or to be held softly like a baby? Know by the messages your body is giving what is right for you and what is wrong.

Meeting each other's needs

Getting close is all about finding out what's right and wrong for you and your partner, and meeting those needs as closely as you can. We have provided an exploration that lets you do this by checking through the ways your partner sees the world — memories, thoughts about himself, what's important, what motivates her, how he understands, future dreams, thoughts and the way they're organized, what colours and sounds she prefers, what makes him feel bad and good.

Using the list we have provided, ask your partner the questions, and note down the answers. If you can, try to see each answer not as a way your partner is different from you, and therefore a threat, but as a way your partner is unique, and is therefore bringing something new and different to the relationship. When you've finished, swap over, so that your partner asks the questions and you respond.

Couples often continue this exploration by discussing their discoveries with each other. If you do, choose a time when you're both happy and relaxed and can cope with any threatened feelings that may come up. A lovely way to finish off is to make a list of all the ways you have (or plan to have in the future) of getting closer to each other — distance dissolvers!

Beginning or continuing a relationship can be like discovering and exploring a new-found world. New mountain ranges, unimagined rivers, and a totally alien viewpoint may challenge you and sometimes feel very strange. Discovering your partner's world may not be easy. But when you've explored sufficiently, and can celebrate the new discoveries you've found, then you can find that appreciating distances can be the best way of getting close.

LOVE STRATEGY 7
Exploration

1. The past.
   What are your three happiest early memories?

   What do you think are your three most important early memories?

   What (if different from the ones you've already spoken about) are your three most upsetting early memories?
   How do you think these memories affect you today?

2. What is true about you — tell me the things you are certain are true, whether I agree with them or not, about:
   your physical appearance;

   your mind and your intelligence;

your personality;

your emotions;

your achievements;

your skills;

3. What is important to you in life?
   What is the most important thing about work?

What is the most important thing about your living situation?

What is the most important thing about leisure time?

What is the most important thing about people?

What else is important to you?

4. What motivates you most to do something?
Fear of what will happen if you don't.   ☐
The thought of something good happening.   ☐
The thought of someone else being pleased.   ☐
The thought of having done your best.   ☐
Other things.   ☐

5. How is it best to explain something to you? (Choose any
combination.)
Talking.   ☐
Drawing pictures.   ☐
Showing you.   ☐
Letting you read a book.   ☐
Letting you try for yourself.   ☐
Explaining the whole thing.   ☐
Explaining little bits at a time.   ☐
Other ways.   ☐
What makes knowledge interesting to you?
The ideas behind it.   ☐
The use you can put it to.   ☐
The way it adds to what you already know about   ☐
something.

6. If you dream of the future, which of these comes up most?
   Achieving good things. ☐
   Having power or influence. ☐
   Being liked by everyone. ☐

7. Which of these is the most important element of a memory?
   (Check with several before you make up your mind.)
   The sounds. ☐
   The images. ☐
   The feelings. ☐
   Which of these is the most important part of a memory
   and which is the first thing you need to think about in
   order to remember the rest of the memory?
   What you did. ☐
   Where you were. ☐
   When it was. ☐

8. Would your ideal environment have
   bright or dim lighting; ☐
   rich colours, pastel colours, black and white; ☐
   loud or soft music; ☐
   fast or slow music; ☐
   hard or soft furnishings; ☐
   coarse or smooth surfaces? ☐

9. What makes you feel good and what makes you feel bad
   in the morning;
   when you're at work;

   when you're at play;

when you're talking to your partner;

when you're making love;

when you're with friends;

when you're alone?

10. What's the one thing we haven't talked about that you really
    want me to know about you?

LOVE STRATEGY 8

Coping with bad feelings

Have you ever seen a porcupine? Large, shambly and covered
with spikes, they have a habit, when threatened, of rolling up

into a ball and waiting, their hands over their eyes, until the danger goes away. Rolled up, their soft vulnerable tummies are to the inside, and their sharp and often quite vicious spikes are to the outside. Two of them, gazing malevolently at each other, can end up as twin prickly globes, side by side in the landscape.

Like porcupines, we too curl up when threatened. Prickles to the outside, we snipe and spit or protect our vulnerable parts with withdrawal. And it often seems that, just when we need to be close to our partner is the time when this reaction sets in, and we set each other off on a spiral of mutual curl and prickle.

I can always tell when Kim is upset about something. She will go very quiet, and take on her 'hunted animal' look. She answers my questions in monosyllables and looks away. I make a conscious effort to talk to her then, and get her to let down the barriers and confide in me. (Paul)

We both have very strong wills, and will not give in to each other. Rose will box me in with logical argument, and I will sulk. I've never known it last beyond the next day, though. (Phil)

We didn't find a single couple who never got upset with each other; we didn't find a couple who didn't have wonderful ways of resolving it.

We are not talking here about relationship-rocking megaton crises in a relationship; those are dealt with in Chapter 13. We are talking about the ways in which we can rub each other up the wrong way, suddenly irritate each other, or end up in a downward spiral of unhappiness without quite knowing why it has happened. This can be part of day-to-day life, even in the most stable of relationships, even with someone you love, even from the very beginning.

Childhood fears

To understand why these things happen, look to the past. Locked away memories of things that have happened, thirty years ago or three days ago, stay in our heads. Locked away feelings about those things stay in our bodies. For when as children, we trip over, see a big frightening dog, or want desperately to go to the party, the emotion rushes through our bodies in response to that pain. Like a fallen-on knee, that memory is stored as vulnerable, delicate, easily able to be scraped again. And if our reaction to the pain — our childhood tears, our fear, our temper tantrums — are stamped upon and shut up tight, then we have an additional emotion, guilt, to concern ourselves with.

The messages of hurt, whether then or now, are twofold. The first are messages about how the world operates. And because they are often based on a child's world, and because they have often generalized from the original event, they are often in-accurate. 'All dogs are frightening, and I can't cope', thinks the female executive who at four, was knocked over by an Alsatian. 'All women will leave me because I'm not worth it' believes the man who at 24, was bowled over by an unhappy love affair.

The other messages are less direct. Often, unless we have parents who let us be frightened and then face the big dog, or friends who held us when we cried about that failed relation-ship, we end up with a legacy of guilt. 'It is bad to feel sad, bad to feel frightened, bad to feel angry.' We know it is bad, for the first time we tried it, we got slapped down, and that hurt.

Then, when something similar happens in the here and now, we forget that we are not in the there and then. 'I just kept remembering being with my first-ever boyfriend, and him dis-liking my body.' says Lucy. 'Every time I tried to make love with anyone else, I just seized up.' For we learn too well when things are painful and make us sad or angry. The next time triggers the feelings we felt the last time. We react that way the next time, and the next time. And often, we feel bad about feeling bad.

So in the day-to-day business of getting close and keeping close, you may not only be dealing with your real interaction with your lover. You may be dealing with your own past history, and his.

Think back. When was the last time when your partner's tone of voice unaccountably jarred you, or his untidiness set your teeth on edge? We have some news for you. There is nothing intrinsically bad in a tone of voice. There is nothing intrinsically good about tidying up. Your next door neighbour, with her past history, would feel totally good about both. What there is, for you, is a video in your head which reminds you of times in the past where that tone of voice made you feel bad, or being untidy accompanied a telling-off from those around you. The present triggers off the memory of the past, and the relevant feeling.

How your partner feels

What you may be realizing, in a flash of enlightenment, is that this is a two-way process. When was the last time you said something innocuous and realized your partner wasn't happy? When did you touch a raw nerve, and get a too-strong reaction? How come you ever get irritated with each other anyway, when you're both trying so hard to please each other?

> When Ian gets down, he needs to be on his own, even if only for half an hour. At first, this would link back in with all my past rejections and the times I'd been left, and I'd get down too. Ian would then feel trapped, because of the way his parents used to hound him, and we'd end up chasing each other round the room, Ian trying to get some peace, and me trying to get close. (Sue)

When triggers are two-way, and what you do triggers what he does which triggers what you do, you may well end up, as we did, quietly chasing each other round the room.

There are many common triggers. Most people feel bad if they hear someone getting angry, even if it is in the adjoining flat, or on television. Most people will react to a friend's tears with sympathy or consolation. But even though triggers are common, when your reactions are triggered, you don't have to feel the way you feel. You can remember that the emotion has built up over the years, and that the partner asking you to do the washing-up can be reacted to in a different way from your father shouting at you to do the same.

Breaking the links

There are ways to break the links. The first way is to realize that no one is to blame. We are all hurt, by design or by accident, and even the most loving families produce offspring who feel painful emotions when they are adult. Knowing this should make us more tolerant of our own emotions, and of our partner's. As he flips into silence because you've lost his favourite album, tell yourself that he's merely curling up into a porcupine ball to protect himself from past hurt, not from you. As you snap because she seems to be taking you for granted, tell yourself that you may be showing your prickles in a triggered response to something that happened a long while ago.

Another way to cope with bad feelings that are about then rather than now is to admit them. Learning to look, listen and feel, as we suggested in Love Strategy 6, should help you recognize when you or your partner is feeling bad. You can see that tightening of the jaw that indicates you've hit the jugular. You can feel that clenching of the stomach that means he's done the same. Why not simply admit it? 'I'm feeling irritated. Can we do something about that?' can stop a problem in its tracks and bring you closer just by being honest.

There is a danger. 'I'm feeling irritated' can be phrased as 'You're making me irritated'. These are not the same words, and the effect is totally different. In the first, you are admitting without apology what your own state is and asking for support. In the second, you are blaming, and that will always cause trouble. For your partner doesn't ever cause your bad feeling. You may not be able to control it, but that bad feeling is yours right back to the hurt that began it.

While admitting your own bad feelings can help if you don't blame, pointing out someone else's will only help if you do it in a very special way. The partner who is feeling bad is probably already feeling bad about feeling bad. Years of messages about the horror of their anger, fear or tears has hammered home to them that if they get emotional, they also get rejected. So tread carefully and lovingly, and only if you are sure that no trace of bad feeling is left in your mind or your voice, feel free to say 'I notice you're cross. Can I help you?' Your partner will hear the words, but if you aren't feeling totally fine she may also hear the subtext — 'I notice you're feeling cross. That makes me feel so bad and angry with you that I have to help you or I'll kill you instead.' Not a good idea.

A better idea is to look at the triggers and out-trigger them. The past-present link works two ways. You can feel bad by re-experiencing something that made you feel bad in the first place. And you can feel good by re-experiencing something that made you feel good in the first place. A classic is the hug. Most of us have lovely warm memories of being held by our parents, and a hug will nearly always comfort or cheer us up. You can get more subtle than that, though. If you know that a particular look, tone or touch helps your partner relax, try that when she's feeling bad. Ian's tension always shows in his back, and a fail-safe relaxer is for Sue to give him back-massage. If you know that for you, a walk in the sun is a good experience, try just walking, conversations banned, next time you both feel down.

Don't pretend

Attempts to cheer up have to be honest, though. Lovers can tell dishonesty at fifty paces, and a mixed message of hugs, massage or friendly walks on the outside combined with bad feeling inside is worse than no hugs at all. Pretty soon, hugs themselves will get linked with dishonesty, and you'll be triggering each other off every time you touch!

Genuine positive experiences are effective though, and often you don't even have to experience them. Sometimes a memory of a time when you both felt good, about yourselves or about each other, can bring the good feeling flooding back. Really remember the best day you ever spent together, the first time you met, the most exciting time you made love, describing to each other what you saw, heard, and felt. If you both join in, and really begin to remember, we challenge you not to feel good afterwards!

Keeping bad feelings away

Once you're both feeling better, there are several things you can do to avoid getting back to bad again. The first thing is to talk over what triggered the bad feeling in the first place. Be careful here, because irritations can be set off again simply by discussing them. So get in a good mood before you do.

> We always talk things through afterwards. We'll laugh our heads off saying 'And when you said that... and I thought...' We're slowly learning what presses each other's buttons. (Caroline)

For if you can find out exactly what it is you are both doing to make each other feel so bad, you can often avoid doing it.

One of the most effective things we've ever found to take the prickles out of a situation is this. Next time you even begin to feel the slightest flutter of irritation, stop, look and listen. What is it about your partner's expression or voice that is triggering your feeling? We guarantee that it won't be so much what he's saying, but the way he is saying it. He may need to be reassured about this, so if you can lovingly explain to him the way you would prefer him to behave — speaking slowly rather than rushing on, looking at you rather than letting his eyes wander — you may be able to avoid potential prickles before they even start.

The alternative is for you to change. Rose's habit of leaving old, mouldy coffee cups decomposing in hidden places round the house used to drive Phil to despair. Then he realized that this was just her way, that his response was based on past experiences, and that anyway there was nothing actually illegal in mouldering crockery. Now he allows himself to play games of 'find the coffee cup' every day or so, and they make a joke of it. Button-pushing avoided on both sides.

In the final analysis, though, even in the stablest of relationships, the feelings may come through regardless. However much you may step outside the anger, or remind yourself that it is only the past talking, you may need to let out some bad feeling, and so may your partner. In this case, allowing them or yourself to do so happily is probably the best answer. Sometimes our bodies need to express emotion. Happily, though, is the operative word. Because for many of us, there are messages about emotion being bad. 'Boys shouldn't cry', 'Keep your chin up', 'Don't get angry, it's not ladylike'.

So it may be that you need lots of reassurance that it is all right to show your feelings, and lots of support when you do so. A word of warning here. Unless your feelings are genuinely nothing to do with your partner, the anger or fear nothing to do with his behaviour, then don't expect the support to come from him. We did speak to people who were able to sit calmly and listen to their partners saying how rotten they were. They had rarely managed it for long, and they had usually worked for years to achieve this security. Instead, find a soundproof room or a trustworthy friend who will let you moan and never ever remind you afterwards of the rotten things you said about your loved one.

These then are some of the ways of avoiding past messages and dealing with present bad feelings. But which of them work for you? We offer you an exploration to find out. The questions are about what you need if you're in a bad state — to be left alone for example, or to be hugged. There may be different kinds of bad states you get in — the long, slow sulk or the short, sharp snap — in which case you may need to offer some alternative answers.

Finding out just what you need to feel better can be a very empowering thing, for then when you do feel bad, you know what to do. A word of warning, though. Sharing the results of your findings with your partner is a lovely idea, but don't expect her to come across with just the support you need if she is in a bad state herself. For irritations often spiral, and she may be in just as much of a mood as you are. Similarly, if you are still angry with your partner, don't try to offer help; even following her instructions to the letter will fail if it is motivated by hidden but nonetheless smouldering bad feeling. So spring to each other's aid when the issue is outside your interaction, or at that time in prickly interaction when one of you is genuinely calm and loving and can say, in the words of one of our workshop couples, 'We can step outside all this'.

A last word is in order, we feel, about porcupines. They are prickly, and they are defensive. They are sharp, and they can hurt. But next time you or your partner plays porcupines, remind yourself of this. Porcupines have very soft, vulnerable tummies.

Fig. 10 LOVE STRATEGY 8 Exploration

	YOU	PARTNER
1. Do you need to be stayed with or left alone?		
2. Where is the best place to be when you are feeling bad? Where should be avoided?		
3. Do you need to be held, touched, stroked, and if so, exactly how?		

Fig. 11 LOVE STRATEGY 8

	YOU	PARTNER
4. If you get really upset or angry, what is the best way to bring your attention back to the present? (e.g. walk you around, tickle you, fight)		
5. What sort of emotional reaction do you want from your partner? (e.g. not involved, feeling with you, angry at the world with you, sympathetic)		
6. What kind of humour will lighten your mood, and what kind pushes you right back in?		
7. Is it best for your partner to agree or disagree with you?		
8. Is it useful for them to point out other people's opinions on what you are upset about?		

Fig. 12 LOVE STRATEGY 8

	YOU	PARTNER
9. Is it useful for them to compare you with other people who are doing worse than you are?		
10. Is it useful for them to point out counter-examples to what you are feeling down about?		
11. Should they concentrate on the past, future or present when comforting you (e.g. tell you how things have been getting better, how it will be different next year)		
12. Which thoughts or memories will unfailingly cheer you up?		
13. How long a time do you usually need to feel better?		

5.

How do you get what you want?

Have you already read Love Strategies 4 and 5? If so, you'll know the importance of being clear about what you want. Preparing for a relationship, choosing a relationship, you have a better chance if you don't leave it to luck.

We've already talked in broad terms about needs and wants; we're now looking at the nitty gritty of success, the practicalities that can doom the best-intentioned of relationships, and kill the liveliest of dreams.

Love Strategy 9 deals with identifying where your individual ideas and ideals, as well as your day-to-day wants and expectations, meet or clash. Is your idea of love the same as his? What is agreed between you about the way you run your relationship — and more importantly, what isn't agreed, but is taken for granted?

There are bound to be clashes. Not crises, just things that need to be ironed out for the smooth running of the partnership. Although other Love Strategies (6 on clear communication; 8 on coping with bad feelings) offer groundwork on this, Love Strategy 10 here gives you a detailed strategy run-down on how to negotiate so that, given that you know what you both want, you have the skills to get it.

LOVE STRATEGY 9

Checking out your expectations
As you begin your relationship, in the first flush of amazement that this wonderful person has agreed to go out with you, you may not be aware of having any expectations at all. Even later,

when once a week has become every day, and the likelihood of your going home even to pick up your clothes has diminished, it may not be an issue. If you marry or commit yourself, then you may begin to think more definitely about what you expect, to make a picture of the future that is, in fact, what you are choosing when you choose this person. But in the main, in love, most of us seem content to take things day by day, happy that in the present, we have found someone who cares.

In fact, like it or not, we do each have a tick list in our head. Before the first date, let alone the first child, we have expectations of what it will be like to go out with, sleep with, marry or retire with, our partner. And, in fact, our partner has a similar tick list. Children? Tick for yes. House or flat? Tick for flat. Who makes the cup of tea in the morning? Well of course he should. . .

The messages of the past create expectations of the present. 'Of course men work', 'She kissed me so she must want it', 'He said he loved me so I know he'll come back'. And many of these are fulfilled. Most couples who marry choose to have children. Most people who kiss go further than kissing. And in partnerships, as in all other relationships — with bosses, friends, relatives and children — we live to a general set of rules which tell us what's going to happen. We buy in to a contract.

What is your contract?
Contracts can be explicit or implicit. In other words, they can be discussed or unspoken. There's no difference in content, no right and no wrong. It's just that some things are talked about, like the marriage contract or the regular Saturday night date, and some things are assumed, like who does the ironing and whether pregnancy means having a baby or an abortion.

> We share all the housework. We're very clear about that, and we discussed it early on. In fact, because of the problems just before we married, we talked a lot of things through prior to the wedding that many couples never talk about. I made certain promises to Rose, and I've kept them. (Phil)

The other thing about contracts is that some are kept to and some are not. Unless it's maintained through fear, the unbroken contract is generally a better option than the broken one. And unbroken contracts are generally the result of a lot of agreement between both of you. You might have talked it through until you were both satisfied, 'We talk everything through compulsively — even which pub we'll go to.' (Pete). It might be so much a part of your background and culture that you are happy with it anyway. You may have begun by disagreeing, but through negotiation (see Love Strategy 10) ended up deliriously content.

Broken contracts can break relationships. And even explicit contracts get broken. 'Till death do us part' vow thousands of couples a year — two out of three of whom will part well before death. 'When I married my first husband, we'd planned to emigrate to Australia' says Nicki, 'Three months later, he'd gone off the idea, but I hadn't. I've always felt cheated.' For people change, and change their minds; what was important at the altar may dwindle into insignificance when the mortgage begins to bite. Then you need renegotiation, sometimes of the contract, often of the whole relationship.

But when it comes to contracts that go wrong, implicit ones are usually the culprits. For your inner idea of a relationship, forged through years of past affairs, may be so unlike hers as to be unrecognisable — and she will fail to recognize the fact, labelling your behaviour at best unreasonable and at worst unloving. If your expectation of what will happen when you're going out (living together, married, pregnant) is not fulfilled, then anger may be followed by disillusionment. Your partner meanwhile, is unaware not only of not fulfilling your expectations, but also of the fact that you even expected her to in the first place.

> We had a special book of pictures of ourselves. It was very personal, and intimate. We'd never agreed not to show it to anyone else, although I suspect I knew we had an implicit contract about that. When Rob discovered I'd shown it to a friend, he saw it as a deep betrayal. (Nicki)

Nicki and Rob left their agreement about the book implicit. So when Nicki acted one way, thinking it was all right, Rob felt the contract had been broken, and reacted strongly. Had their contract been explicit, they would not only have had a chance to talk it through and agree on secrecy, and the importance of secrecy, they would also have been able to cope far better with one or other of them breaking the contract. For who can be sure they're not in breach, when no one's quite sure what they're in breach of anyway!

Working out what your contract is strengthens any relationship. It's a good exercise to look at what's happening, and it avoids avoidable rows. One of the couples we interviewed had actually written down their contract.

> Before we married, we decided our agreements. A lot of them were about money, but some were about resolving rows. We each wrote out our agreements, signed them and kept a copy. We redo them from time to time, though it hasn't been necessary for a while. (John and Terri)

The exploration we offer you as the main part of this Chapter is to do just what John and Terri did. We've provided you with a series of questions about the main areas any partnership takes into account, explicitly or implicity — areas such as work sharing, money, sex and futures.

The first step in doing the exploration is for you, and your partner if you have one, each to go through the questions alone, answering each one.

If any of the questions aren't relevant to your situation — you aren't living together, you aren't sleeping together, then you will still get useful information by imagining what you would expect to happen. If you really can't imagine this though, put 'not applicable'. We suggest that answers of a few words are probably enough, but write as much as you need. For each question, put what your *explicit contract* is if there is one (what you have clearly and openly discussed with your partner) and what your *implicit contract* is (the one you think holds, but haven't actually discussed). Times, places, real facts are useful, because they are more objective than ideas. So 'We make love twice a week, and I usually make the first move' is easier to work with than 'Sex is very important to us and we really enjoy it'. Equally, some questions are open-ended and demand fairly open-ended answers. 'Who cooks?' could be answered by 'I do' or 'He does', but might also need the qualification of 'Unless he's really tired, or we've just been to visit my Mum.'

If you haven't a partner

If you haven't got a partner, look over your answers and then chat them through with a friend. Which of your expectations are probably going to be universal ('I expect to have sex with my partner') and which will be specific to you ('I couldn't bear my partner to have to work'). The specific ones may be areas you will need to check out with future partners, because they may be ones they're not expecting!

Compare notes
If you have a partner, the next step is to go through the questions one by one, noticing where your answers are the same, and where they are different. This can be a difficult thing to do, as you realize that your expectations of the relationship are different from your partner's; so take it slowly and be prepared for lots of discussion over some points. You or your partner may say 'But that's not what happens' or even 'But that's not what I meant to happen'. Remember that when you find a mismatch, you also have an opportunity to talk through, negotiate and sort it out. Better to find out now than when it's caused trouble.

The point is that differences are not desperate. It doesn't mean she doesn't love you if her view on money is not yours. It doesn't mean the relationship is doomed if his ideas of fidelity are not yours. It simply means that your partner's experiences have been different, giving him different expectations of the common bond we call love.

Once the exploration is done, you may find the balance of your relationship changes as you both adjust to the new knowledge and the new situation. And, once done, this swap of expectations does need to be redone regularly. Ideas and ideals change, and many a relationship has foundered because the common view you started off with has turned into one where you both gaze in opposite directions. But given time, a lot of discussion and some skilful negotiation, you may both score full marks on each other's tick lists!

LOVE STRATEGY 9
Exploration

Housework

Cooking

1. Who has the responsibility for cooking?

2. How often do you expect that you/your partner should cook?

3. Under what circumstances do you expect to have a meal cooked for you?

4. Under what circumstances does your partner expect to have a meal cooked for him or her?

Cleaning
1. Who has the responsibility for cleaning what?

2. How often do you expect things to be cleaned?

Shopping
1. Who has the responsibility for shopping for
    (a) food?
    (b) clothes?
    (c) other things?
2. Who decides what to buy?

Repairs and maintenance
1. Who has the responsibility for general repairs?

2. Who decides whether to get a specialist in?

3. Who organizes getting a specialist in?

Gardening
1. Who has the responsibility of doing which job?

2. Who plans improvements?

Earning a living

Workspace
1. If you work at home, what if any rights does this give you to take the space you want for working?

2. Do you have separate workspaces in the house, and if so what are your agreements around this?

Decisions

1. How do you expect to make decisions for one of you to change jobs/apply for promotion/go on the dole/get further education etc?

Interest

1. Whose work do you expect to talk about most?

2. How much interest do you expect to show in your partner's work?

3. How much do you expect them to show in yours?

Emotional support

1. What right do you have to support when things are difficult at work?

2. What right does your partner have to support?

3. How should that support be expressed?

Money

Earning
1. Who do you think has primary responsibility for keeping the money coming in?

Spending
1. Who has the responsibility for deciding on
   (a) general budgeting?
   (b) particular items?
2. How much can you spend without checking with your partner?

3. How much can your partner spend without checking with you?

Deciding

1. How do you expect to make major financial decisions?

2. How do you expect to decide between alternatives when there isn't enough money for both?

3. Who has responsibility for deciding
   (a) how to pay bills?
   (b) how much you afford on luxuries?
4. Who keeps track of the bank account/mortgage etc?

Keeping

1. How much do you expect to save?

2. How much is it all right to borrow?

3. How do you decide where to invest your money?

Environment

Outside
1. Who takes the responsibility for deciding which area/kind of dwelling you live in?

2. What are the important factors in that kind of decision?

Inside
1. To whose preferences do you expect to decorate and furnish the home?

2. Who takes responsibility for doing that?

Other people

Parents

1. What responsibilities do you each have to your parents?

2. What responsibilities do you each have to each other's parents (e.g. visits, care when growing old, care of surviving parent.)?

Other relatives

1. What responsibilities do you each have to your other relatives?

2. What responsibilities do you each have to each other's relatives?

Friends

1. Do you expect all your friends to be joint, or is it all right to have separate friends?

2. How do you expect it to be handled if you don't like each other's friends?

3. Is it OK for your partner to go out with friends but without you? If so, how often?

4. Is it OK for you to go out with friends but without your partner? If so, how often?

5. How often do you expect to see friends to keep up contact?

Life decisions

Marriage

1. If you are not married, under what circumstances would it be appropriate to marry?

2. If you are married, what would have to happen for you to divorce?

3. What would be the most important changes in the contract if you were/were not married?

Children

1. What if the woman gets pregnant — how do you expect to decide whether to have/keep the child?

2. What do you expect the duties of each parent to be towards children (or grandchildren if relevant)?

3. What if the child/children were twins, or mentally handicapped, or physically handicapped, or another man's/another woman's?

4. What if you found out you were unable to have children?

5. What if your partner found him/herself unable to have children?

The future
1. Who will make major life decisions in the future?

2. What will the course of your life be as you grow old?

Communication

Honesty
1. What secrets do you expect to keep from each other (e.g. presents, lovers)?

2. What secrets should always be shared?

3. What sort of thing is important enough to need talking about?

Resolving differences
1. How quickly do you expect disagreements between you to be tackled?

2. Where and when do you expect disagreements not to be discussed?

3. What are the rules for coming to agreement?

Emotions

Showing emotions
1. Which emotions is it OK for you to feel?

2. Which emotions is it OK for your partner to feel?

3. Which emotions is it OK for you to show to your partner? What about in front of others — in public, with friends, parents, children?

4. Which emotions is it OK for your partner to show to you? What about in front of others — in public, with friends, parents, children?

Thresholds
1. How bad do you expect to feel about something your partner is doing before mentioning/challenging it?

2. How bad do you expect your partner to feel about something you are doing before mentioning/challenging it?

3. What's the best way to deal with bad feelings?

Time

Together

1. How much time do you expect to spend together at this stage in your relationship?

2. How much time do you expect to spend together at later stages in your relationship?

Apart

1. How much time do you need alone?

2. How much time does your partner need alone?

Sex

Together

1. Which of you makes the first move?

2. When and where are/are not appropriate times and places for sex?

3. What is/is not OK for you in sex?

4. What is/is not OK for your partner in sex?

5. Do you expect to talk about sex or ask for what you want?

6. Do you expect your partner to talk about sex or ask for what he or she wants?

Outside the relationship

1. How far can you go with someone else?

2. How far can your partner go with someone else?

3. What would you do if your partner stepped beyond that limit?

4. What would your partner do if you stepped beyond that limit?

5. How would you go about changing this contract if you wanted to?

Changing tastes

1. How would you respond if your partner wanted a gay/hetero relationship?

2. How would your partner respond if you wanted a gay/hetero relationship?

3. How would you respond if your partner wanted to experiment with other sexual tastes — bondage, rubber, unusual (to you) positions etc?

4. How would your partner respond if you wanted to experiment with other sexual tastes?

LOVE STRATEGY 10

Negotiating to meet both your needs

The scene is the middle of the desert. There is a large, high, stepped pyramid. On each side of it, sitting waiting, are two people. They can't see each other, but they can shout. The words we hear, as they occasionally yell across, are things like. 'I'm not moving. I want to go east. You come over here.' 'I like it this side, west seems a good direction. Why don't you move?' They were on a journey across the desert. But now they seem to have got stuck.

When you have a difference of opinion with your partner, often you can end up one each side of a seemingly unsurmountable barrier. This may be a crisis, something that threatens to ground your relationship, or it may merely be a short break while getting your relationship off to a flying start. You know you are right in your view, your plan, your needs. So does your partner. Impasse.

Well, not quite. There are ways out. One is to unfailingly put your needs second and your partner's needs first; many people, particularly conventional wives or henpecked husbands, choose this route. Another way is to skilfully and artistically throw a temper tantrum whenever you don't get your own way. If your partner will allow this, it never fails — and only a vague feeling that perhaps there is more to life than crockery-throwing and partner-trampling may disturb your peaceful nights. A third way, which may be the best if there are too many impasses, is to find another relationship. Or at least, if every fight for your needs ends up as a death struggle, leave your present relationship.

Negotiation

We believe there is a better way. It's called negotiation, and it's a way of getting you up from the sand so that you stride off again across the desert, both in the same direction.

Negotiation is taking each of your needs and finding a point where they overlap and meet. Then, when both of your needs are met, a solution should follow. It takes some skill, and it is an acquired taste, but it is worth it. When properly handled, it avoids the temper tantrums, ignores the temptation to give in, and increases love. For who can fail to love their partner more when, all the time, the partnership is giving them more and more of what they want? Both ways.

We negotiated our relationship from the very beginning. Each of us had very particular needs about how the relationship was run, and about how much time and energy we committed to it. So before we even agreed to go out together, we negotiated. Over the years, the original needs have changed; we now have no limits over our commitment to each other, but we do sometimes feel oppressed. But we still say that everything is negotiable — except the basic principle of negotiation. (Sue)

So you are a person, part of a couple, that is prepared to negotiate. Think what that says about you. It says that you are committed to your own happiness, and your partner's. It says that you are not prepared to compromise on either. It says that you care enough to go for equal meeting of needs, not a win-lose situation.

Check this out with your partner first. Agree that this is a good thing to have in your relationship tool box, and certainly very handy when it comes to the big things; 'We never agreed to have children. We just did it. I wish now we'd talked it through' (Eleanor and Frank). It can ease off your relationship in small things too; you can negotiate over which pub to go to, what colour the curtains will be, or whether you'll spend an hour or two hours visiting your parents.

Once agreed on the basic principle, there are some safety regulations to observe before you start pyramid climbing. The basic one, on which all others are based, is — don't bother if you're feeling bad.

First things first!

It's impossible to negotiate, or even communicate, when the emotions are negative. In physical terms, your body puts all its energy into coping with the feelings, and has none to spare for even trying to see anyone else's point of view. So the first thing to do if you both feel bad is to stop trying to tell each other anything. Concentrating instead on feeling better will not only restore the emotional balance and decrease the possibility of nuclear war, it will also hasten the time when you can both sit opposite each other once again and actually summon up any interest in what the other person wants.

Take a break, give each other a genuine hug, think of times you've felt really good about each other — use all the skills you may have picked up from Love Strategy 8 — to get back into a good space. We have been known to play ring-a-roses round the living room before, and during, a particularly difficult negotiation!

The best thing, of course, is to use negotiation to outflank the bad feelings by getting in first. If you can negotiate promptly and effectively whenever one of you feels your needs aren't being met, then the chances are you'll never get to feel bad about the cooking or afraid about the way she drives. 'There's a marvellous feeling of security about our relationship now' says Maggie, of her recent use of negotiation in her partnership with Simon, 'We know that sooner or later both our needs will be met, so we don't need to get het up about it.'

When and where do you negotiate? There can be formal negotiations, a kind of Camp David agreement taking eight hours in bed or all day Sunday over endless cups of coffee. Or, once the skills are learned, it can be three minutes outside the Odeon, on what film you're going to see. Places and times can matter — choose ones where you both feel good. Ric and Maria always negotiate things in the car, an ancient Morris. 'It seems to be linked to resolutions now. So much so that the other day some friends asked us if they could borrow the car — not to drive, but to negotiate in!'

What is the issue?
You are sitting, then, in a good place at a good time, feeling confident of a resolution. Or in other words, one each side of a pyramid, aware of the barrier, but ready to decide a direction. What now? First, share with each other what the issue is. You will each have your position. 'I want to go east,' one will say. 'I prefer west,' replies the other. Be it which house to buy, which car to drive, whether to get up early tomorrow, how to make love, whether to make love, you will each want to go a different way.

But why do you want to go that way? Any issue, any direction is an expression of need. And needs can be much broader, much more understandable than simply 'I want to'. Do you want that particular house because it is big, or because it has a garden? Do you want to get up early in order to get the shopping done, or so that you see the sunrise? Picture the two desert people at last climbing just one step up the pyramid, willing at least to communicate now. 'I want to go east because there is a town there.' 'I want to go west to see more of the desert.'

Needs stated, you may still see no hope of meeting them. Your partner's needs may not be your own because of his way of looking at the world. So your need for a garden may clash with his need for a garage. And your need to get the shopping done may clash with her need for more sleep. 'I don't want to see the desert.' 'I don't want to visit that town.'

What then? Remember that there is no blame here, and that your partner's need for something you don't need is just a sign of his uniqueness. But in fact your longing for a garden and his desire for a garage is based on a much deeper need. What is it? You might love a garden because it means the children won't play in the street; he might want a garage because caring for the car may save the family money. And it might be that this is a little easier to understand or identify with. Another step up the pyramid, another move closer together. 'I understand that you want to get the shopping done so that we can go to the park together today.' 'I understand that you want to sleep in because you've been so tired every evening this week.' 'You want to go to the desert because it makes you feel peaceful.' 'You want to go to the city because it makes you feel excited.' Ah.

Reaching an understanding
What you're aiming for, and it may take hours of talking, is to reach a point where the understanding is total. Where without compromise, or a feeling of giving in, you can look at your partner and say 'Yes, I understand your reasons and your needs. Let's find a solution that meets them as well as mine.' Then you're getting somewhere.

Up the pyramid, step by step, finding needs beyond needs until you discover ones that are compatible. You realize, in a sudden burst of sympathy, that saving family money is important because he actually does want to give the children the best possible life. And this is a strange and wonderful coincidence, because that is important to you too. You really need a house with a garden so that you can relax in the evening — he might even be able to see that as your way of supporting the family by being more relaxed with them.

And going to the park is actually not all that important — the real need is for you both to spend some time together, and that's why you want to get the shopping done. Which is actually not too far away from the fact that she wants sleep to give her more energy for the relationship. That makes you feel a lot better right away.

'I realize that feelings are important to both of us. You want to feel peaceful, I want to feel excited.' 'Yes, and why do we want that — I want to share a deep emotion with you now we're together.' And up to the top of the pyramid they climb, step by step.

It could be that that doesn't happen. Given strong feelings, or the realization that for one of you, sticking to your position is more important than reaching agreement, the negotiation can break down. If this is so, whether you are the breaker or the one left with half a negotiation hanging in the air, you need something else. If your partner stops, halfway up the pyramid, and refuses to continue, what do you do then? Ultimately, the answer may be 'I'd rather finish the relationship than suffer this.' But when it's worth it to you to continue, make sure you have another alternative. It could be resources of your own, money to put towards a garden, a spare room to sleep in. It could be the strength to take your own direction, off towards the rising sun. But you need to know that, if you fail to reach the understanding that the best negotiations aim for, you have another option than just giving in.

Changing attitudes
Once you've got agreement, and your outcomes in general are compatible, although in specifics they are different, the feelings will change.

> When we first met, we kept clashing about whether to go out in the evening or not. Eve kept pushing for us to stay in, and I kept imagining quiet evenings in front of the telly and feeling bored. It was only when we really talked about it that I realized her idea of an evening in was wine in bed! I always remember that feeling of relief when we understood each other. We laugh about it now. (Trevor)

Once you are in agreement, you can begin to find a solution that satisfies both your needs. Occasionally it will be one or other of the directions you originally proposed. More often, it will be a completely different third that meets both your needs. The house with a garden, not a garage, may turn into a house with a garage backing on to a park; or a house with a garden and a car port. If giving the children a good life and supporting the family are the central issues, there are lots and lots of ways to do this.

The morning-rising may turn out to be a question of working out times. If you both get up later then she will get her lie in, and can then run you both to the supermarket. Or you can arrange to do the shopping on Friday night. . . or Saturday afternoon and drop in to the park on the way home. . . or eat out all weekend anyway. The important thing, you've both established, is to be happily and energetically together.

How can you learn to do this too? A first stage is to get practice in finding out the needs behind the issues. Using the grid as a guideline, you can write down something that is an issue for you — with your partner, a flatmate or a friend. Then find the need behind the issue, and write that down. What's the need behind that? and behind that? Don't worry if, in the end, you come to an enormously broad need — to be loved, or to survive. This is where most of our needs end, and if we realized this at the beginning, we probably wouldn't have to negotiate anything with anyone. We'd both see the need and understand.

If you have a chance to take this exploration further, then get your friend or partner to do the same as you have done, over the same issue. Compare notes. When you reach a point where you both understand and feel good about each other's needs, you can start to work out a solution for both of you. Start by each deciding on three solutions that you think might meet both your needs, then see if any of them satisfy you both. If not, then it may be that you are simply not communicating because the time, place or mood is not right, in which case, do something about that. Otherwise, look at what other needs you have that haven't been acknowledged — do you need to take them into account? Finally, brainstorm other possible solutions; it may be that you simply haven't hit on the right one yet.

Negotiation skills are useful, even though they need practice. Ideally, everyone would use them to start, maintain and end all relationships; because they take time to learn, it's tricky using them only when the relationship is in trouble. Most formal negotiations take place at the divorce stage — about thirty years too late. Instead, start now, learning to meet the needs of both of you in all your situations. Like most insurance policies, it will pay dividends in the end.

Meanwhile, back in the desert, the two desert people have reached the top of the pyramid. Talking, exchanging needs, beginning to understand, they have finally ascended step by step, to the summit. And of course, on the summit, they have no choice but to stand side by side and face each other. 'I realize now that we both want emotions.' 'We both want the same thing.' 'How can we get excitement and peace together?' 'Do you think the top of the pyramid is big enough?' 'Well, it might be — are you thinking what I'm thinking?' 'Yes — and afterwards, I believe there's a town in the middle of the desert over there . . .'

Fig. 13 LOVE STRATEGY 10 Exploration

	You	Your friend/ partner	Are these needs compatible?
What do you want?			
What will having that get you?			
What will having *that* get you?			
What will having *that* get you?			
What will having *that* get you?			
What will having *that* get you?			

WHEN YOU GET AGREEMENT THAT THESE NEEDS ARE
COMPATIBLE

Suggest three solutions *each* that you think might meet the
needs of you both.

Which of these six is the best solution?

6.

Me or you?

Someone's 'other half' or your whole self? Being in a partnership can pull you in two different directions, from hanging on to your own identity to slotting neatly into a pair. But which to choose?

What we've learnt from the people we've talked to is that it's a question of balance. Two individuals, each clinging on to their egos for dear life, means the death of any relationship. On the other hand, sinking gently without a trace into the lifestyle, the personality and the priorities of your partner is just as fatal.

The two strategies we offer you here are not as clearly separate as the others because they look at the same issue — identity — from two different viewpoints. Successful couples seem to use two strategies for solving the same problem, maintaining and valuing their own individualities as well as identifying with the relationship in a way that allows them to understand and support each other. To do this in an integrated way is like breathing in and out. Incidentally, we see these two strategies as the keys to success in love.

Love Strategy 11 suggests ways you can value your partner's individuality and freedom as well as celebrating yourself and the contribution you make to the relationship.

Love Strategy 12, the complement to this, looks at how it is possible to identify with your partner, take their view of the world and use that skill to enhance the partnership.

Taken together, the two strategies suggest that, with relationships at any rate, two into one will go.

LOVE STRATEGY 11

Maintaining identity within the relationship

The relationship begins. For a while, there is nothing more

wonderful than spending time together, sharing accounts of
your days, ringing each other four times a day and at bedtime.
But as the security grows, as weeks become months, and plans
span years, a strange thing begins to happen.

You begin to want to be alone again. Just for an hour after
coming home from work, just for a day to wash your hair and
sort your clothes out. 'At first we didn't even go out without each
other. Now we're starting to recontact old friends again, and
have evenings alone.' say Pete and Caroline. And this is
happening to your partner, too − this need to be alone to
recontact the feeling of being self-sufficient.

We're not talking here about the tell-tale signs of a flagging
interest, the disagreements, the rows, the hesitant excuses and
the last-minute cancellations that signal the end of things. We're
talking about the natural need of all of us, however much in love
we are, to maintain our own identity. For we are all individuals.
That is what attracts us to each other, that uniqueness that
makes one complement the other, and fit so snugly into a pair.
We all have our own line in lifestyles, and we all need to know
that we are enough on our own, even though being on our own
is not enough. So although you still want to be part of the partnership and all its rewards, you also want to keep your own self
intact.

> I know that being independent is very important to Eve. She really
> needs to feel that she has her own thoughts, her own feelings, her
> own self. I am very careful not to stifle her too much, to give her lots
> of freedom. Otherwise I think she'd leave. (Trevor)

Giving each other space
One of the main things we found successful couples doing was
giving each other lots of opportunity to develop and celebrate
this special sense of self.

Why should you do this for your partner? Because you love
him, and that's what will help him be more of who he is. That's
one, selfless answer. Another more pragmatic one is that if you
don't, you and your relationship will suffer. A person who only
likes herself in the context of a relationship with you, a person
who can do nothing without asking permission, a person who is
merely a reflection of yourself, is not a partner, she's a ghost.
Also, given time, she's a resentful ghost, a deceiving ghost, or an
absent ghost.

We're not talking here about happily standing by and allowing your partner to trample all over you with size ten boots. If you aren't getting what you want in a relationship, talk, negotiate or leave. We're talking about the dangers of needing your partner so much that you can't let her out of your sight, and needing her to be so like you that you can't let her out of your control.

What attracted you to the other person in the first place was her otherness, her particular specialness that gave you what you needed and complemented you perfectly. If, in the end, she loses that, you are losing out; and if in the end, that difference begins to threaten or jar, remember that that was why you chose her.

> I liked Pete first of all simply because he was thoughtful and sure. I felt secure with him. He really liked my spontaneity and bounce. Then we started driving each other up the wall because when it came to taking decisions on the house, we were so different. I expected Pete to think through things at the same instant rate I did, and he got annoyed because I made snap decisions. It took us a while to realize that that was what had got us together in the first place! (Caroline)

One exploration you can do is to write down all the things that originally attracted you to your partner, from his green eyes to his sense of humour. Stick to the positives, and add any more that you've discovered since you first met. Then list five things about your partner that seem to impinge on your identity or self-esteem. Don't dwell, but be specific: 'His untidiness', 'She has no sense of timing'. Then go back and work out if any of the things you feel uneasy about actually stem from things that, in the beginning, you did like. Are any of your pet hates a direct result of what makes your partner the person you love?

Remember, too, that the total package that is your lover is what allows you to function as a unit. If any of the bits were missing — even the bits that rub — you might not form a complete whole. We have very different ways of reacting around people. Sue likes to be liked, and puts a lot of energy into building good, friendly relationships with people. Ian, more direct, will happily challenge someone if he feels that it will help them or him in other ways. 'I'd have no friends left if it wasn't for Sue.' 'And I'd get walked all over if it wasn't for Ian.' We think we do better together than separately.

Letting your partner know how you feel

You may by now be a little more aware of your partner's strengths, and how these strengthen the relationship. But does your partner know these things? So often, the messages we hear from our partners are about how we could be different. If you're close to someone, you often tell them where they're wrong, sometimes because you're irritated, often because you feel they need to hear it. What they probably need to hear too is where they're right. Past messages of worthlessness can be so loud that it takes a lover to shout over them. The joy of the first months of a relationship is celebrating each other's wonderfulness, but we often forget to repeat the procedure at regular intervals. Partners, like plants, need regular watering to remind them to grow.

A reminder, too, about needs. Doing the implicit/explicit contracts exercise in Love Strategy 9 may focus attention on the fact that your partner has different needs from yours. If so, and you can meet these needs without compromise, then it is a good long-term insurance. Someone who has the time she needs to herself, the space to be alone when he needs it, the freedom to be with other friends, doing other things where appropriate, will be happier to come back home at the end. 'I realized that without occasional evenings out alone, I may well end up needing occasional nights away with someone else. Joe agreed, and I now spend time on my own, at the theatre or just walking.' says Katie.

Being close can mean being too close. It can mean forgetting that your partner is not you, and starting to treat him as if he were, making your priorities his and his life your responsibility.

> James was really into physical fitness. Almost as soon as we started going out, he encouraged me to go to keep-fit classes — and I began to realize that he was keen for me to go because he identified with me. It took a while before we worked out that I had my interests and he had his — and that because I wasn't going running didn't mean that he wasn't keeping fit! (Helen)

If you can realize that your partner literally does inhabit a separate world from yours, with a different past history and different messages floating round her head, you may begin to understand why she acts differently. And understanding, to allow her to move through her world while you watch lovingly from yours.

Keeping your own identity

But if your lover needs and deserves to keep her identity, then so do you. An equal partnership is made up of equal people, and all that you've just read about your partner applies to you too. If you owe it to your partner, you owe it to yourself. Double.

Allowing yourself the opportunity to develop and celebrate your special sense of self is sensible in many ways. You'll be more of who you are and who you want to be, and you won't end up resentful, deceiving or walking out because you're not a person any more, just half of a couple.

For you too, contribute to the whole by being uniquely you, and if you lose that uniqueness, to become a shadow of your former self — or of someone else — then the partnership as well as you will suffer. So become aware again, if you've forgotten, of what you have to offer, what originally drew your partner's attention to you that day in the pub. Look back to the celebration chart in Love Strategy 2, if you did it. Get your lover to remind you, with no qualifications, ifs or buts, of what attracted her to you in the first place. Work out together what you alone contribute to the relationship. What special qualities do you (and no other person) have that makes the partnership so special in itself? 'I know I'm the one person who could support Malcolm,' says Jane, 'I really feel I've helped Dave work through his sexual problems' says Tom.

This self-congratulation need not be a one-off. Remind yourself constantly when you've done something well, contributed something, really helped. Ask your lover, if she's willing, to point these things out too. Rope in your friends, your Mum, the girl at the next desk. It will raise some eyebrows, but a genuine congratulation a day will keep doctors, psychiatrists and divorce solicitors well away.

One of the hardest things to do, though, is to wipe out of your mind past messages of failure such as we talked about in Love Strategy 2. 'For years I couldn't bear any lover saying good things about my breasts,' says Julia, 'because my first lover thought they were too small.' Remember that the things you really remember are often the worst, not a representative sample. How many appreciations have got lost under the memory of that one put-down? Revise your memory, and raise your self esteem, by realizing how much you may have forgotten.

If your present happiness is still threatened by a sharp comment in the changing rooms ten years before, remember that you're a different person now. How would you have reacted then if you'd known, experienced, loved, what you have now? What would it have been like if you could have used all your present skill and sensitivity to cope with that past situation?

And do yourself a favour by treating yourself to lots of good things. Just because you have a lover who pampers you (or doesn't) does not mean that you can't be good to yourself. People we talked to mentioned massage, an afternoon in the sauna, a good book in bed, new clothes, delicious food, good wine — all for yourself and enjoyed by yourself. You don't have to be with your partner to indulge. Use the exploration to brainstorm as many ways as you can of being good to yourself.

And, just like your partner, you too will have needs — needs of time, space, evenings to yourself or with your friends. There is a temptation to think that loving means never wanting time to yourself. On the contrary, really giving to someone else may mean you need more time for you, to integrate what is happening. We drove each other mad during the first months of living together by feeling we were failing by not interacting every moment of every day. Now we read over meals, have occasional times away from each other, and feel a lot more relaxed.

For while loving may mean losing selfishness, it shouldn't mean losing yourself. Your relationship should make you prouder of yourself, more aware of your own identity. Your own personal hope and fears, likes and dislikes, needs and wants, should all be able to fit within the context of the relationship you have.

> I've always been wary of relationships, in case I end up being someone's 'other half'. But I know now that I was a whole person before I met Trevor — and that I still am. (Eve)

Fig. 14 LOVE STRATEGY 11 Exploration 1

Things that attracted me to my partner
  1.
  2.
  3.
  4.
  5.
  6.
  7.
  8.
  9.
10.

Things about my partner that now impinge on me

	Which attraction they relate to	What the connection is
1		
2		
3		
4		
5		

LOVE STRATEGY 11
Exploration 2
Ways of being good to myself

Things I can do for my body

Things I can do for my mind

Things I can buy myself

People I can see

Things I can tell myself

Things I can congratulate myself for

Things I can treat myself to

Time I can give myself

Space I can give myself

LOVE STRATEGY 12
Identifying with the relationship

Having an 'other half', be it spouse, cohabitee or friend, can be a secure, safe feeling. Or it can be very worrying. For other halves can all too easily be just that — 'other'. The person into whose eyes you lovingly stare can very easily take a totally different point of view, and the partner who fits so snugly round your body can very soon grate and jar on your mind. Familiarity may not breed contempt, but it can very soon lead you to a sense of alienation.

Two different people, attracted to each other because of their differences, may very soon find these very differences repel. He loves playing sport, while you find it too competitive. He considers political involvement necessary, while you find it useless. Yet you get on well, have good sex, love each other deeply. So what's the problem?

It can be a real problem. 'We get on superbly but I can't understand his need for freedom,' says Dave, of his year-long relationship with Tom. 'It isn't the way I would act if I was with someone I loved.' Faced with real differences in the way you see the world, it is very easy to get irritated and frustrated. Why doesn't this person react as I do? Why can't he see things the same way? Snappiness, anxiety and direct rows can be the result of trying to present a unified front to the world and at the same time trying to integrate another mind and personality into your own.

If the struggle is too much, and the people are too different, one person may realize it's not right, and break off. Often, though, the joys of having a relationship keep you in it, trying to integrate no matter how much it hurts. And here perhaps the people who care most hurt most, because they will be the ones who keep trying to force octagonal pegs into oblong holes until the mould breaks.

Internal conflict between wanting the relationship to work and trying to accept someone else's individuality impinging on your own is a natural outcome. 'I swung from blaming him for being a bastard to blaming myself for being too intolerant. It took me a long time to realize that we just didn't fit,' says Diana of her first husband. For, real cruelty aside, bastards and bitches are often not the people themselves, but the fact that they don't meet their partner's expectations. A bastard is all too often someone who doesn't want what you have to offer; a bitch is more than likely a person who wants someone else. No blame; different worlds.

One solution we found for many of the successful couples we talked to was that of being able to identify with partners — literally to enter their world and understand what was going on for them. This wasn't something that successful couples did all the time; some didn't do it at all, others only sometimes. Everyone who did it kept a balance between identification and individuality. But the identification was there.

Enter your partner's world
What is this identification? What happens, what does it feel like? It's more than just the being close we've talked about before. It is entering into your partner's world so fully that you almost become him. You understand his mind, you feel his emotions.

> Sometimes we end up practically thinking the same thoughts. We'll approach things the same way, get angry or tense at just the same time. It's as if we are living in each other's bodies sometimes. (Maria)

The power of being able to do this is that when you do, it can make disagreements and misunderstandings very hard to sustain.

> I just couldn't bear to hurt Rose. I hate to think of doing something that might upset her. If I consider it, I feel bad — I suppose I feel what she would feel, and I just couldn't do it. (Phil)

Phil not only realizes mentally that Rose would feel bad if he did certain things. He literally feels her feelings, identifying with and understanding her reaction so totally that it would be very difficult for him to do anything to hurt her, because he would actually hurt too.

How does this identification happen? The first prerequisite seems to be that the relationship must be worth it. It seems to be something that couples develop with time, as the relationship means more and more to them. 'I see the relationship as being the most important thing — more important than any issue between us, or any strong feeling of mine.' says Ric. Getting close to your partner is something that you may do in the first stages of a relationship, when like a child with a new toy, you are wide-eyed with wonder at this unique person who is wide-eyed at you. But to survive getting to know someone, to survive the sheer habituation of spending time with them, the relationship has to be important in your life. If it is, then you have the motivation to begin to identify with your partner.

If you have a common outlook, you have a head start. Opposites do attract and complement, and it is fascinating to share stories of how totally different your childhoods were. But people with no common experience can find it difficult to understand how this other, alien mind works. Far better if you know that what you value, what you aim for, what you notice, will be valued, aimed for, noticed by you both. Arranged marriages often work because of this — the careful choice of partners from the same world, to marry and live in the same world, with the same world view. 'We're both from up North,' say Caroline and Pete 'and so we have that Northern sense of humour. We fall about laughing when everyone else is wondering what's going on.'

Building on common experience

Whether common background is there, from the moment you meet, common experience will be. From the first glance, you begin to build up an archive of joint knowledge, places you've both been, things you've both done; 'Darling, they're playing our song' — ours because we were both there, and in love, on one occasion it was played. If the relationship develops, so does the archive, to include love-making, rows, break-ups, make-ups, mortgages, children and pensions. Each experience adds to your common fund, and your knowledge of the other person.

Common knowledge isn't the binding force, of course. Golden wedding couples have been known to divorce, and forty years can seem thirty-nine years too many. The force only binds when every common experience gives you a little more understanding, makes you a little more able to identify.

You don't have to wait forty years to learn this skill, though. You can understand your partner's viewpoint and feelings easily and quickly by simply asking. The early days of a relationship usually allow lots of identification because they allow lots of talk of yourselves and how you feel. 'I love you' she says. 'I know how you feel — I love you too,' he replies. And to some extent, in the wonderfully emotional climate of falling in love, they do. Later, as the practicalities of shared beds, shared rents, shared children take over, it's somehow not quite as acceptable to talk about each other. Feelings get stored, like the early photos, and the question 'What are you thinking?' is answered with details about the garden, not about your mind.

So ask. And if asked, tell. What are you thinking? How are you feeling? Use all the skills you may have learnt from earlier Love Strategies to explain to your partner all about the pictures in your head, the memories in your brain, the feelings in your body. 'I'm feeling tense in my stomach. I keep imagining the MD's face at the meeting tomorrow, and hearing him shouting at me,' will allow your partner to feel more of what you are feeling, and react much more supportively than 'Got a bad day tomorrow. Need a drink.'

You may have done the exploration in Love Strategy 6 which suggests that you listen to your partner talking and understand his world. The next stage on from that exploration is this. Take it in turns to pretend that your partner has achieved overnight fame, for being just who he is at present; same job, same home, same situation. You are a film actor, whose job is to play this celebrity in a re-creation of a day in his life. Of course in order to play the part, you need to talk to the celebrity, find out how his mind works, find out how he would react in this situation or that, find out particularly what emotions he feels, so that you can portray him on film. Ask all the questions you need to in order to really get inside this person and, like any good actor, feel what it is like to be him. Don't just stop at knowing from the outside what your partner thinks and feels. Do it with them, taking on and trying out their reactions and emotions. It can leave you amazed at how your partner's mind is put together, and amazed that you never realized before.

Seeing your partner's point of view
With this experience, you also have the skills to move on to real understanding, even during crises, even at times when you feel very far apart. Try this next exploration by discussing a decision you and your partner disagree about. At first, choose something you disagree about happily, in order to feel good while exploring. The questions take you through your partner's way of thinking and feeling about the issue so that you begin to experience it like they do. They help you to ask 'How would I have to think; what pictures would I have to make, what voices

would I have to hear, what feelings would I have to feel in order to experience it like you do?' Incidentally, it's quite difficult to stay angry with someone when you can see their point of view as clearly as if it were your own. Done both ways, this is the one of the strongest techniques we know for resolving arguments.

> After the workshop, we started exchanging viewpoints more and more. Then one day in the middle of a disagreement I said 'Tell me how you're getting angry'. I imagined thinking and feeling the same. It was so overwhelming we both cried. (Lucy)

There can be problems. If you see the world through your partner's eyes all the time, you can lose sight of what it's like being you.

> I was quite afraid of sleeping with Simon, because I thought that once we had made love I would be overwhelmed by him, his ideas, his personality. I'd lose myself because of loving him. (Maggie)

Maggie needed to be very sure of her own identity before she could allow herself to get close to Simon. She knew that if they did anything as binding as make love (which can create the strongest bond of all) she would start to identify with him. Many people, particularly women, feel this way. If they really get close to someone, there is a very real fear that their ideas, their ideals, their way of seeing the world, will be taken over by the other person. It is a danger, and you need to be careful, keeping your own identity separate and unique.

Another danger is this. If you really understand and can 'take on' your partner's viewpoint, you will also take on his behaviours. This is the whole point of opposites attracting — the fact that if we are with someone who has what we have not, and we get really close to them, we take on their thought patterns, their outlook, their reactions. 'Now I'm with Rob,' says Nicki, 'I've started to hoard things, just like he does. I'm sure I wasn't like that before!' So you can end up taking on your partner's weaknesses, becoming just as stingy as she is, just as lazy as he is, developing just as ulcer-forming a lifestyle as hers.

You need to be able to stand outside your partner's limitations, seeing why she does things, but choosing not to do them too if that's not right for you. Also, if it's not right for her. The most wonderful thing in the world can be someone so inside your experience that he cries with you. Someone so inside your head that he shouts when you shout and gets depressed when you do is not helpful.

But otherwise, with your self-identity safe and your partner's weaknesses secured against, why not identify? The 'you might end up like them' argument works both ways. Who wouldn't benefit from spending time with a caring partner, and learning to care, or being with a partner with a natural capacity for contentment, and becoming more content yourself?

Though we never found a definitive definition of 'love' for the other person, the idea of really understanding and identifying with your partner was the nearest we got. 'I know I accept Kim because I never need to question anything' says Paul 'I understand why she does things, so it's all right.' 'When I think of doing something for Phil, I imagine how good he's going to feel when I've done it, and just jump for joy.' says Rose.

Step inside your partner's mind, map in hand. Walk around for a while, looking and listening. Feel the surge of excitement, feel the twinge of anxiety. Appreciate, maybe for the first time, the worry of getting it right, the sheer joy of making friends, making a sale — all the things that are real for your partner, and may be totally alien to you. Experience all this, knowing that every time you do so, every time you understand a little more, you make it more likely that you can help, support, sympathize. You make it more likely that you'll make the relationship work. So why settle for one view of the world when you can have two?

LOVE STRATEGY 12
Exploration

Questions to ask your partner about some decision you disagree on.

	Course of action you favour	Course of action I favour

The future

1. What do you imagine happening?

2. How clearly can you imagine it?

3. Which option is most vivid in your imagination?

4. Which option is most detailed in your imagination?

Self-image

5. What would accepting each option say about you?

Other people

6. Which other people's opinions or responses are important in this?*

7. What are these opinions/responses?

Feelings

8. What do you feel when you
   think of each option?

9. Which of questions 2-7
   gave you the most powerful
   response (feeling)?

* Of course, if your partner is identifying with the relationship,
  then you are probably no longer 'another person' to him, but
  part of the relationship you are both in together.

7.

How do you cope with crises?

Thinking of problems in relationships almost always means thinking of crises — infidelity, money problems, constant rows. In fact, one of the most encouraging things we learnt by talking to people was that this sort of crisis can actually make a couple more, rather than less, successful. So crisis is not the end of the world.

But it may seem so at the time. Love Strategy 13 offers an analysis of what happens in a crisis, some ways of pulling back from the brink, and some solutions aimed at solving the issues which precipitated the crisis in the first place. As well as this, there is a chance to plot the course of your own pattern in crises, and look at ways of interrupting the crisis path where that's appropriate.

We didn't find a relationship that didn't have crises. It seems that if two people are attempting to work as one, there must be times when there are impasses, and the future looks bad. Otherwise you never really realize what it is you are fighting to save.

LOVE STRATEGY 13

Coping with crises

Crises, like thunderstorms, come in many varieties. They can start slowly and grow gradually, or blow up overnight. Small niggles, huge megaton rows, days of silence and hours of screaming, walk-outs and lock-outs and break-ins. It seems that even the successful relationships — perhaps *especially* the successful relationships — have times when the whole thing seems in peril, destined to go up in a cloud of smoke. Yet, like the phoenix, successful relationships have a habit of rising from the ashes, in spite of and maybe even because of — the problems.

For a relationship threatened can become a relationship refined. A crisis can help you to realize what you might be missing, and also realize what is missing in the relationship, and supply it. A relationship under threat can force you into rethinks and renegotiations, and the end result can be better than ever. A crisis may be nature's way of telling you that you can do better than this, and you can do it now!

> A short while before we were married, I confessed to Rose that I'd been having an affair. She was horrified, and in the ensuing quarrel, break-up and renegotiation, we cleared up a lot of things between us. We really had to be totally honest, and go for what we really wanted if we were going to be able to carry on. I made Rose some promises then, and I've always kept them. I honestly believe our marriage was better because we faced up to that before. (Phil)

Crises don't have to be about infidelity; in a brainstorm of 'issues' in one workshop we ran, things mentioned ranged from money through sex, children, each other's parents to personal cleanliness! And in fact, the issue that triggers the crisis is often not important. Who does the cooking may not be an issue for you; for some people it can be the cause of their splitting up. For crises are not about what; they're about how — how they're triggered, how they happen, how you cope with them!

In this strategy, we deal with all sorts of ways to cope with crisis. Slot your own personal issues into what we're saying.

How a crisis develops

Crises, just like storms, need the right climate to develop. This climate is very often the marriage of two alien minds that suddenly look at one another and say 'What on earth is that?' For, as we've explained in earlier Love Strategies, the fascinatingly different person glimpsed across a room can become the threateningly different person impinging on your life. It can seem as if the closer you get, the more difficult it is to be truly close. Because your partner is unique, he does things differently and finds different things important — and that can seem oppressive. And if you try putting your standards on to him and treating him as if he was your double, he can feel oppressed. Mike's initial attraction to Cathy as the mother of two children turned to anger when she put their needs above his. Love Strategy 12 suggested identification, but if this doesn't happen, the result can be alienation. Irritations can soon mount up. One sarcastic joke may pass unnoticed, whereas the sixth one can have you reaching for the meat cleaver. And if your present partner has exactly the same line in put-downs as your past one (or your mother), your tolerance threshold will be much lower.

People do notice the bad things more than the good. The things that made you tingle when you first met your partner — the particular colour of her eyes, his kindness, her laugh — become day-to-day normality. You begin to take them for granted. The horrors, however, work differently. Each one scrapes the old scar, and irritation piles on irritation. And so the climate for crises develops.

The climate established, an initial trigger, large or small, sets things off. This varies from couple to couple, but one thing remains constant. The bottom line is that when your partner cannot or will not do something you want her to — be that to stay faithful or to do the washing-up — then crisis ensues. For no matter how much we love, and how much we care, if the climate is ripe for crisis and what we are getting is wrong, we will fight to the death to get our needs met.

From the initial trigger, things can take different courses. Each course can be very different, and we only mention a few that can be developed, explored, and put together in different combinations.

The first thing to look for is whether the crisis is affecting both of you, or only one of you. In some ways, you must both be involved, but often only one partner feels the crunch and the other is left unmoved. 'I'm usually the one who flies off the handle,' says Sue. 'Ian is usually very cool. But when he does get angry, I can often stay calm just because he's not.'

And there can be spirals, where you sense something intangible in your partner's voice which unaccountably makes you tense which automatically triggers him into irritation which then makes you angry which. . . and so on.

Recognizing a crisis
As you start to realize that you're moving into crisis mode, you

may begin to recognize certain signals from your body. Feeling tense, tight in your stomach or shoulders, a little weepy or even very tired. All these are signals that something is not right.

If you experience something you don't like, your internal pictures and sounds can also change instantly.

> When we're building up to a row, I picture Maggie, not smiling, not looking at me, distantly as if I'm seeing her through a glass. Once things are resolved, I imagine her much more clearly, as if the glass is gone. (Simon)

> If I notice Ian doing something I don't like, a voice inside my head comments on it, in a very irritated way. 'He would do that, wouldn't he', or 'Oh, not again!'. When I'm feeling good about him, I don't hear those voices. (Sue)

What happens then? It can all result in silence. 'Liz just goes quiet for about fifteen minutes if she's upset. I can't talk to her then, but eventually she comes out, and we resolve it.' says Kathy. If your way of coping with a flood of emotion about your partner's behaviour is to keep quiet until you feel better, then you've developed an elegant love strategy — with two ifs: if you take care that the issue you got angry about gets resolved; and if you take care that those feelings aren't popping up somewhere else in your life — in your series of motor accidents, for example, or your sudden bouts of migraine.

Defence mechanisms
It is possible not to feel, and if feeling bad about your partner threatens a relationship that is vital to you, then your body may choose not to feel. As soon as something sparks it off, it battens down the hatches and retreats into anaesthesia. This is how many partnerships founder; after twenty years of child rearing and seeming the 'perfect couple', divorce ensues. When every-one wonders why, the partners admit that it's years since they 'felt anything'. The first few times of irritation were bad enough — they stopped feeling after that, and got on with the business of looking after the kids. And only a fresh young lover, or a bright new job could make them feel again, remind them of what they were missing, and push them out of the door.

Next stage up from anaesthesia is maybe selective deafness or blindness, the ability to screen out what you don't want to know.

John couldn't hear when his first wife called him, simply because the sound of her voice wasn't something he wanted to hear. Celia didn't notice when her lover was less and less interested, because it wasn't something she wanted to accept.

Or you can be a martyr. It is possible to avoid a crisis by simply not allowing it to happen, by feeling but not showing your feelings, by agreeing with your partner and supporting him whatever happens. There are disadvantages to this (such as migraines, eczema and cancer) for unresolved needs have a nasty habit of making themselves known in one way or another. And if the only way they have of getting you to realize that there's something wrong with your relationship is to put you in hospital, they may well do that. A less drastic but maybe more frightening disadvantage to continuous 'yessing' is that your relationship will never get the chance to improve. If you know that one challenge to the partnership will sink it, then choose carefully. If you're happy to stick with that situation for the rest of your life, fine. If not, maybe it's better to sink now, and swim away while you're still young enough to float!

But not everyone sticks with it. Some remain silent but let their feelings out in subtler ways. 'I never say a word,' says Debbie 'but it's strange the way meals get overcooked when he's late home.' Some people talk things out, but with hidden agendas about attacking.

> We can't really make progress for a long while after we begin to argue. Up to then we both want to win too much to be able to communicate, or even feel like calming down. (Phil)

Some will snipe, where the comment is harmless but the tone of voice is pure vitriol or where the tone is honey and the remark is vinegar. This 'war of attrition', as one couple called it, can go on for days, never quite erupting into open battle, but nevertheless leaving you both sullen and shattered.

One not-so-delightful way that this can go is that one or both of you will end up playing polarity. Whatever your partner says seems wrong to you. So you polarize from it, disagreeing, contradicting, saying the opposite, and then if your partner should chance to agree with you, saying the opposite to that. You aren't being deliberately awkward a lot of the time; it's just that some part of you is determined to prove that your partner is wrong, and so contradicts whatever he does. Two people playing polarity, each denying what the other is saying or trying to do, can end up playing emotional volley ball of the most destructive kind!

Bad feelings pile up

It can become unnerving, the inevitable way that each of you affects the other. Bad feeling stacks upon bad feeling until it is uncomfortable to be in the same room as each other. Although there may be no outward signs of tension, you have simply had so many uneasy times together that some part of you takes one look at your loved one's expression or one listen to her tone of voice, and wants to be somewhere completely different!

Then at some point when bad feeling triggers bad feeling triggers bad feeling, one of you will go over a threshold of tolerance, and say something. Voices begin to rise shrilly, or soften with tears. Shoulders can tense with frustration or slump with despair. Words that you never thought you'd say come out at top volume from your mouth. And words you never thought you'd hear are flung at you, along with a packet of self-raising flour, as one couple told us!

And there you are in a full-scale row, often not knowing quite how it happened. It can be in public, though it's more likely to be in private. It can vary wonderfully from time to time. 'Don't expect consistency' says Nicki and Rob 'we can be different people at different times.' Do expect to feel powerfully, and badly, about your partner. And do expect the time to vary too. Short sharp lightning flashes, daily repetitious thunder crashes or storms building up for days; they can be dramatically different from person to person and row to row. Yelling, throwing, fighting, walking out and slamming doors; you will have a wonderful range of ways to wind each other up.

And you will learn to row with each other, and change your ways of rowing as you learn about each other. 'When I met Ian, I'd sit on my anger for hours, scared to raise my voice.' says Sue 'He called it my "frightened rabbit" expression. Now I'll yell loud enough for the whole street to hear!'

Another way feelings can change is that bad feelings can spread. This is essentially the way relationships die; what was a totally good experience can, by the addition of enough bad feelings, become a totally bad experience. Nasties generalize, and what was an objection to her arriving late can become a series of objections to her spontaneity, her informality and her ability to live in the present. The crisis moves from a mild irritation to a flash of anger, to days of silence, to the divorce court.

How do your crises move? It can help a lot to chart the way they go and, if possible, compare your view with that of your partner. Armed with this information you can then work out ways to manage the crises as they happen.

The exploration we offer consists of questions to guide you through charting the progress of a crisis in your relationship. Fill it in on your own at first, and let your partner do the same if he's joining in. Then compare notes, realizing that as you remember crises you have had, it's all too easy to slip back into that frame of mind, and end up in another crisis! There's a lot to be learned not only by analysing what you see happening during a crisis, but also what your partner sees happening. Often the differences between the two are a lesson in themselves!

Getting out of a crisis
Having looked at how you got into a crisis, we look at how to get out. And just as every couple has their own way of feeling bad, so each couple has their own way to feel better.

The first question to ask yourself is 'What do I want?' Of course, you may immediately respond, 'I want to resolve the crisis'. In fact, a crisis of any sort, be it a row at the breakfast table or pistols at dawn, is a sign that somewhere, somebody needs something they're not getting. But what?

It could be a divorce, and it could be that all the reconciliations and couple counselling in the world will not stop that partner's inexorable progress to where he wants to go. If this is you, read Love Strategy 14 and 15, and if you want out, don't bother wasting time with the crises — you don't need Acts 1 and 2 if what you're really interested in is the finale.

It could be that what you want is something your partner can't give you. From a swimming pool in the garden to a compliment on the dance floor, from a wedding ring to a baby, people do have limitations on what they can give. If you aren't getting what you need, you have three choices; change your needs, change the way you're going about getting them, or change the person you're trying to get them from. Later on, we'll be suggesting some ways to get your needs met, but if your partner really can't oblige, then you may have to alter what you want — or read Love Strategies 14 and 15.

If you know your partner can give you what you need, but just isn't doing so, then you have more of a chance. Check out first that what you think you want is really what will satisfy. Is it his agreement to go to the theatre on Saturday you're concerned about, or a much wider-ranging agreement to spend more time together? Is it her attitude to money you want to change, or just that particular tone in her voice when she mentions it?

It's useful too to work out in advance what will satisfy you. Many a crisis has lasted longer than it need because one or other of the protaganists has got what they wanted but not realised it!

> I was looking for reassurance and was convinced that the only way she could give it was by saying she would stay the night. In the end she couldn't because she was on shift, but when I got upset, she was so loving that it reassured me anyway. (Kathy)

Once you know what you want, the bottom line is not even to try to get it until you are both feeling good. Communication, discussion, negotiation will all fall to pieces if you attempt them when one of you is still reaching for the hand grenades — and if you start negotiating in a good state, and mention of the issue sets either of you off again, take equally drastic avoiding action.

To do this, there are a variety of things you can use. Many of them have been mentioned in previous love strategies, particularly number 8, to help you through the perilous waters of setting up a relationship. But here's an action replay, along with a few more heavy-duty techniques. All are relevant whether it's you, your partner or both that are unhappy.

Anything that normally makes you feel good can help — making a cup of coffee, playing a hard game of squash. Any place that makes you feel good can help — our favourite is standing at the window of our high-rise flat, looking out over London. Anything that reminds you of good times can help — memories of a day at the seaside with your parents, or a day in the country with your partner. Any reminder of your own strength is a good idea — the time you comforted your best friend or had the guts to stand up to a tyrannical boss. Really remember these times, in your head, or share them aloud, recall every detail of what you saw and heard, and every feeling that you felt.

Anything that really changes your focus of attention can avoid a crisis. 'Emma, our daughter, is great at stopping us arguing — she'll just ask "Why are you shouting Mummy?", and we both start laughing.' say Rose and Phil. Changing the focus of attention by physically getting away from each other was a favourite one for many couples — although as Paul says 'I hate it when Tom needs to be alone in order to get back in a good state. I feel locked out of his life.' One couple felt better by telling each other jokes!

There are lots of things you can do in your mind to change the way you feel. 'We often imagine we can see ourselves rowing — from the outside. We sort of step out of the picture and see these two people screaming at each other, and it looks so silly we stop.' say Helen and James. Ric has another way of looking at it.

> I get really hooked into an issue or something I want. Then after a certain point, I start seeing in my mind's eye a picture of Maria and I together, and the picture gets bigger and bigger, as if it's far more important than the issue we're arguing over — and I stop arguing. (Ric)

You can also change the triggers. Most people are triggered into anger by someone else's angry signals, and for one of you to genuinely feel better and take on a relaxed voice tone, suddenly seeing the row as interesting rather than upsetting, can alter the whole course of the interaction. 'Snap out of it' can seem a heartless suggestion when you are in the midst of emotion, but if you can change emotional gear, then your partner will find it impossible to stay in crisis mode.

Dealing with the issue
You're feeling better. You are at last meeting each other's eyes when you look, and feeling at least able to begin to listen when your partner speaks. What now?

Now deal with the issue, if there is one. What do you want to be different? What does your partner want to be different?

> I really need to talk everything through. It drives Malcolm nuts, but if we don't, I feel a sort of twisted resentment, and it's no good. As long as we've talked things through, they feel better. (Jane)

Over and over we heard couples speak about needing to talk

things through, to communicate both sides of the story, and for neither partner to take sides. Many couples just need to talk through an issue, to understand the other point of view, before they can resolve what they're feeling. And couples need to resolve issues if they are to avoid recurrent crises.

Really identifying with and understanding your partner's point of view, as we explained in Love Strategy 12, can often remove the last traces of anger. Next time you are feeling really close, choose some particular thing that your partner does that annoys you slightly — but not one that sets all your teeth on edge, or you'll end up pulling flick-knives on each other. Use the exploration from Love Strategy 12 to ask your partner to explain just how she comes to do this, what she fears will happen, what she hopes to get out of doing it, how she feels. As she explains, take your time in imagining that you are her, that her values are your values and her past history is yours. It is very difficult to row with yourself.

More formal issues may suggest more formal means — like negotiation. Big things in any relationship, even if they are not crises, work better if they're negotiated anyway: working, housing, kids, money; all the things that can trigger even a saint into defensive retaliation. And even little things, if they get your hackles rising, can benefit from a comfortable negotiation over a large whisky. Love Strategy 10 tells you more about negotiation, in big things and little things.

If you find you can't negotiate, if in fact the more you push for a settlement, the more your partner resists, there could well be something else going on. For we did find, time and time again, that the more one partner wanted something, the more the other partner was against it. In this situation, we're not advocating that you give up your demands and happily let your partner trample all over you. But if you do notice this dynamic, this mysteriously increasing 'no' to what began as a perfectly reasonable demand, then you may be dealing with more than just an issue. Your partner may be feeling threatened, and so the more you push, the more they will push back, to keep the balance of the relationship even. And you can even be grateful that they are not settling for a relationship where they give in when it's not right for them, that they value you enough not to need to placate you all the time. The fact still remains though, that the issue will not be settled until you back off, allow your partner to know that he is more important to you than what you want, reassure him that it is safe to give sometimes.

Recurring crises

It happens that the issue is settled, but the crisis goes on. If you find that you are hitting the same problem again and again, or feeling hugely bad over little things, then look below the top of this iceberg. What is making it impossible for you to negotiate or to identify with your partner? Ask again what you really want — is it what you discussed and agreed on, or is it in fact something different and much more tangible? Are you asking for more money when what you want is commitment? Is she asking for more time when what she wants is fidelity?

It could even be that the bad emotion itself is getting you what you want, and feeling better or resolving the issue is actually counter-productive. If you get more attention from your partner when you cry than you do at any other time at all, then it makes perfect sense to keep crying. And if shouting at your partner gets the reaction 'All right, I'll do what you want', there's no reason for you to stop shouting. There is every reason in the world for your partner to stop doing what you say, because she feels oppressed — but you're doing fine. So if the bad feelings themselves don't clear up, or the issues keep recurring, wonder whether you're actually doing better by having the crisis than by avoiding it.

> My getting ill so often was actually a binding force for us. It allowed me to take time off work, and spend time with Tina — and it allowed her to give me the attention and care that otherwise I was too independent to let her give me. (Alan)

If this happens to you, find out what you're getting through feeling bad, and then think of other ways of getting it instead. Could Alan arrange to spend more time with Tina, and allow her to look after him more, without having to get ill? Can you get the reassurance you need from your boyfriend directly without having to make him jealous? Can you get the support you need from your wife by asking, rather than by being unhappy all the time?

Unhappiness that stretches beyond issues is usually a sign that other things need exploring. If so, you need to look back, and forward, over the whole of this book to find out where you need to change things.

There are several things we've mentioned which might need changing. Is it that you're not communicating, not really able to find out who you are simply because you're not talking about it (Love Strategy 6)? Perhaps you are tripping each other up simply because you are too like people in the past who also tripped (Love Strategy 2). Perhaps, quite simply, you are not the people that each other want, or you have both developed in different directions, and no matter how you try, making the pieces go together will never be an easy fit unless one or both of you changes — and maybe not even then (Love Strategy 5). Perhaps you are not taking enough separateness, but getting lost in each other so that some part of each of you is shrieking for independence, and is starting you rowing in order to get you some time on your own (Love Strategy 11). Perhaps you simply don't know enough about each other to begin to identify with the relationship, so that when it comes down to it, you can't yet meet each other's needs (Love Strategy 9).

Look back over the crisis chart you did earlier in the chapter. Can you spot any points where a crisis could be stopped by using some of the things we've suggested? You can talk this through with your partner, but it is possible for you alone to decide to halt a crisis in mid-track by doing something yourself.

This book is really just a beginner's manual to understanding relationships, and it can't begin to cover the really subtle crises, the dances that people play that actually get them rewards, but also cause pain to themselves and others. We know other things about how to deal with crises, and so do many therapists, counsellors, priests, Mums, Dads, friends and personnel officers. If you need support, reach out for it.

Remember that a crisis is just that — a crisis point along the way. It may be a way to no relationship, or a way to an amazingly good relationship. People we talked to had found that feeling bad made them really get down to improving their relationship, that rowing had given them more energy to put into their relationship — even that splitting up for a while had made them realize what their relationship was and could be. A thunderstorm can be a catastrophe, bringing half a forest crashing down with it, or it can be an energy-raising experience, clearing the air and leaving the atmosphere clean, fresh and ready for a new start.

LOVE STRATEGY 13
Exploration
Climate

Place
Where can you/can't you have a crisis?

Time
If you were to plot crises on a calendar, would a pattern start to emerge — e.g. regular intervals, time of year, just before or after some other event in your lives?

How long do crises last?

How long does it take to build up to a crisis? Are there definable stages?

Triggers

External factors
Outside the two of you, what can set off a crisis?

Actions
What can either of you do that is bound, sooner or later, to trigger a crisis?

Does your partner have a particular tone (or tempo, or volume) of voice that sets off warning bells in your head?

Does your partner have a particular expression, posture, way of moving that signals trouble for you?

What expectations does seeing/hearing these signals induce in you?

How does this affect your own voice or expression? (You may need to check this with your partner — and be prepared for some surprises!)

In full swing

Progression
If you were to plot a graph of how your feelings change through the course of a crisis, what would it look like?

Rules
What is the limit of behaviour beyond which you really would lose your partner?

What is the limit of behaviour beyond which your partner really would lose you?

Patterns of behaviour
Would an outsider see patterns in your behaviour during a
crisis, such as one of you always blaming and the other
placating, both blaming, taking turns to blame and placate, etc?

Hidden agendas
During the course of a crisis, do you find yourself doing or
saying things, less to make a point or defend yourself and more
to
(a) punish your partner?
(b) give yourself 'bargaining chips' for a later negotiation?
(c) in order to force a break-up?

Do you experience your partner doing any of these things?

Note: Your experiences of these two questions will undoubtedly
be different!

Resolution

Subtle signals
What do you see or hear in your partner that lets you know that
it will be over soon, even before you start to make up?

What do they see or hear in you?

After-effect
Are you left with residual bad feeling, or is the after-effect of a crisis more love than before?

If you were to chart your feelings after a crisis, what would the chart look like?

Content
If the crisis was sparked by a disagreement, which comes first — resolving the feelings or resolving the issues?

8.

How do you split up?

In books, plays and films, ending a relationship is seen as the end of the world. It's only really worthwhile if it heightens the tension before a reunion of lovers, or frees one of them to unite with someone else.

In real life it's less simple. Some of the people we talked to spoke of sad partings from past relationships. But many of them saw endings as positive, the natural result of a partnership that was naturally short-term. Also, many of them spoke of gaining a great deal from the process of splitting up, and moving on to other things and other people — or getting back together again with a new strength to make it work.

Love Strategy 14 deals with the problems of deciding when to leave — deciding when staying is best, though painful, and when leaving is painful, though the only alternative. We also look at the long-term effect of short-term split ups.

If the right thing to do is to leave, how do you make that positive? And if you are the 'left', how do you survive? Love Strategy 15 offers some ideas on positive breaks, and ways to prepare yourself for whatever is next in your life. Consider which is better — to stay in a relationship that is not right for you or your partner, or to leave and head for blissful solitude or another love?

LOVE STRATEGY 14

Knowing when to leave and when not to leave

A relationship that is going well has its own easy rhythm. It's maybe a little quicker in the high, speedy first months, maybe a little slower in the gentle fortieth year. It flows along of its own accord, easy and certain. It's good.

But when the rhythm begins to falter, and the cracks begin to appear in what was once the foundation of your life, then you need to think hard and long. Sometimes the problems may be obvious; screaming rows, long absences. Sometimes they are subtler and more insidious: getting tense, getting ill, working late — and wanting to.

The symptoms can vary, but what is constant is the ever-widening gap between what you need and what you are getting. If you need someone to have fun with and your someone gives you only tear-stained discussions and late night phone calls; if you need someone to have a family with and what you have is good sex and nothing in common, it may be time to think about leaving. Or changing. Or negotiating. Or at any rate, deciding what to do.

But how do you decide? In this Love Strategy, we offer you an exploration that is a whole strategy long; a way to work through the decision, step by step, until the issues are clear. Fill in the chart as you go, and see what you discover. In the end, it's up to you, but we can offer some ways to help you make up your mind.

Look at your options
The first thing you can do is to look at your options. Going may be at one end of the possibilities, staying may be at the other. What's in between? Going, but still sleeping together? Staying, but renegotiating everything from scratch? Moving out? Moving in? Moving house? Like a pools coupon, the permutations are endless, and the more you find, however insane they seem, the better chance you'll have of the right jackpot.

> We tried living together when we were first married, and we drove each other up the wall. So when I started my course, I lived in the hostel, and that gave us some independence and a chance to look at what was happening. Our friends thought we were mad, but when I moved back in again, we'd changed enough to make it work. (Maggie)

It may be that all the options you listed look odd. For like new territory on a map, you haven't explored them yet, haven't yet found out what they are. You need to wander, look around, ask questions, find out where you are and where you want to be.

You can ask friends or relatives. But take care. Some friends are to the break-up of a relationship what the Roman crowd was to the gladiatorial combats. Blood excites, and people do get excited and horrified by the thought of other people splitting up. Of course, their horror may centre on themselves, for if Shaun and Tricia can split up after twenty-two years, so can they. People will identify with you, or with your partner. So if you're the one who's thinking of leaving, prepare too for the coup de grace — being blamed. You may know your reasons, your problems, the sheer impossibility of keeping anything going, but those people who identify with your partner won't sympathize with you.

But some of the most helpful advice can come from those people who know you and love you, and want to see both of you happy, whether that means breaking or remaking love. 'No wonder you're irritated with each other, 'a friend once told us. 'You're working like slaves — I'm just surprised you haven't had nervous breakdowns, let alone rows!' If you have such friends, sit them down with a large bottle of chilled white wine, and ask them to be the all-seeing eye. No judgements, no advice, but a clear account of what they see from the outside. Ignore the temptation to ask them what they would do in your place. They aren't in your place, they have neither your problems nor your possibilities, and for that reason, they shouldn't be asked to endanger a good friendship by giving you advice you may later regret or resent.

More objective, less dangerous than friends or relatives are the professionals — therapists, counsellors, help-line people. 'We gulped at the thought of going to see our marriage guidance counsellor' say Collin and Shirley 'But she's helping us a lot.' Getting yourself sound, trained help like this doesn't mean you aren't big enough to cope on your own. It means you're mature enough to call in an expert. There are many people who don't trim their own hair because they can't see round the back, yet will happily try to sort out their own relationships.

Basically, though, information gathering needs to begin at home. Look at your partner, and listen to him. His own inbuilt sense of self-preservation may already be at work, leaving him less likely to phone you, more likely to fall asleep on you. For Robin, it was realizing that Maureen was mysteriously forgetting to write down dates with him in her diary that made him understand that she was losing interest. Some partners are abandoned kicking and screaming, but have actually been pushing away the loving hands for months.

Stop and think

What about you? Your own survival mechanism may already be propelling you towards the door, or towards a more permanent seat beside the fireplace. So don't only look at what you *think* you think and feel, but examine carefully what you actually want. 'Early on, I kept thinking we must split up,' says Eleanor, 'and then I caught myself one day telling someone what "we" would be doing in a year's time.'

You may be thinking of stopping the relationship, but know instinctively that it is worthwhile carrying on, even for a while. Or you may, while believing you are closer, actually be distancing yourself from your partner, letting overtime or evening classes come between you, beginning to imagine a future elsewhere. If ending your relationship is going to be difficult, involving disappointment, distress or divorce, your conscious mind may not want to tell you what your real needs are. Its surreptitious signals may go unnoticed, so stop and think.

Perhaps one of the most powerful 'stop and think' strategies that we learned of from couples, was to up and leave. Somehow it is very easy, close in, to see the worst; hairs in the basin, pans in the sink, unsatisfying communication or an unsatisfied sex life can all blind you to the real delights and opportunities your relationship can offer. Further back, you can see them.

> We broke up about a year after we'd started going out. It lasted a week. I found myself thinking of all the things I'd miss out on in the long-term by not being with Jane. It was as if, while we were together, I could only think of the short-term problems, and splitting up allowed me to readjust the focus of my life. We got back together and got married. (Malcolm)

For when all the pictures of the future are of the pans, or of sullen stares, who can blame you for wanting to exit as soon as possible? Apart, you can begin to remember the laughter, the weekends in bed, the glorious future, and realize the horror of a future without them. And when you do get back together, if pans start to rear their ugly heads, so also does the horror of a partnerless future, and you work harder to stay.

It can work the other way, too. When Shaun and Tricia, participants in one of our workshops, imagined being apart, they began to see the advantages of that; two months later, they achieved a parting that was right for both of them.

So one section of our exploration is about imagining you have ended your relationship. If you choose to do it, really imagine what you would see and hear and feel without your partnership, and particularly without your partner. For feeling bad about having no one can be solved by finding someone. Feeling bad about having lost this particular person can only be solved by hanging on to him now.

Imagine yourself in the future, having split up. What do you miss, being without this person? What are you glad to have missed out on? What do you celebrate now she has gone, and what do you mourn? How has your life changed — the home, the job, the friends, without this person in it? And how do your visions of the future look without this person in them?

Often what people need in order to make a nearly-made decision is to know that they can cope with what they really want to do. So what do you need in order to go — more self-esteem, a place of your own, the certainty of keeping the kids? And to stay — the promise that you'll start making love again, the knowledge that you can cope, or the realization that she still loves you? Phil found that what was stopping him ending his unhappy marriage was the fact that his parents liked his wife so much. Once he had talked it through with them, and knew they understood his reasons, he was able to go ahead with the break-up.

Changing the relationship

'I'll stay' can be harder to say than 'I'm going' if you think that nothing will change. The thought of endless arguments or continuous silences is a crushing one even when you have the brightest resolutions about the future. The relationship must change, you know that. But how? The next section of the exploration looks at that.

You need three things. The first is support. Support from friends who don't mind you being one-track minded, from colleagues who don't mind you being absent-minded, from professionals who will listen, from amateurs who will look after you for a weekend while you sort yourselves out. The support you need might not be people, it might be the cash to move out of your parents' house, or someone to do the cleaning. 'We've always had help in the house,' say Frank and Eleanor 'We think it saved our marriage.'

The other two things you need are these: a willingness to change from your partner, and a willingness to change from you. For if things remain the same, given any amount of second honeymoons in Crete, things will actually get worse. And you will, given a week, a month or a year, find yourself back at square one, contemplating the same question — shall I leave?

Things can change. We've seen them, with ourselves, with people we've spoken to. Horrendous crises can save marriages, and couples on the brink of divorce can later celebrate euphoric ruby weddings. But if one of you is all the time thinking 'Do I really want this?', then save your time, your energy, your breath and your love for better things.

A new beginning
An ending will mean a beginning. The beginning of a bad time, maybe, but then good times. Good times of being alone, good times of finding someone better. Remember that every minute you waste in a relationship that's wrong for you is a minute taken away from the one that's right for you. Splitting up can be the sign of success, if it marks the natural end of a relationship that has run its natural course.

When the rhythm of a relationship is broken, the question is whether it can be started up again. If the answer is yes, if the beat is steady and one you want to move to, then do it. But if all the attempts in the world are just going to result in a sad, stumbling, dying rhythm, then maybe you're better off with silence and stillness.

LOVE STRATEGY 14
Exploration

1. Brainstorm the future possibilities for your relationship.
   Any idea will do, however mad.

2. Ask other people:

Fig. 15

People		Opinions
Relatives		
Friends		
Colleagues		
Professional help		
Other		

3. What does your partner feel about the relationship?

What does he say when you ask?

What have you noticed her doing/saying that is
consistent with this?

What have you noticed him/her doing/saying that is inconsistent with this?

4. What do you feel about the relationship?
What do you say when asked?

What have you noticed yourself doing/saying that confirms this?

What have you noticed yourself doing/saying that contradicts this?

5. What would it be like if you split up?

How would you feel (positive/negative)?

How would it affect your life:

work?

living situation?

free time?

people?

other?

What would you miss if you split up?

What would you gain if you split up?

What would your worst future be?

What would your best future be?

What do you think would happen to your partner?

6. What would you need in order to go?

7. What would it be like if you stayed together?

What is your worst fantasy?

What is your best fantasy?

For each: how would you feel (positive/negative)?

How would it affect your life:

work?

living situation?

free time?

people?

other?

What would you miss if you stayed together?

What would you gain if you stayed together?

What would your worst future be?

What would your best future be?

What do you think would happen to your partner?

8. What would you need in order to stay?

LOVE STRATEGY 15

Making splitting up a positive experience

When life is first beginning, a single cell divides into two. What has been a whole splits, slowly but inexorably, into two halves, which in turn grow to become whole themselves.

When the end of a relationship comes, whether you choose it or it is forced upon you, it can seem like the end of everything. By the time the decision is taken, you've often been through pain, disillusionment and a total loss of self-esteem. And by the time you know, for certain, that this is the end, it can seem as if the ending will be just one more distress as the climax of a whole series of unhappinesses.

It doesn't have to be like that. The whole that was the relationship can divide easily and creatively into the two halves that first came together. Becoming single again, you can regain the singularity that you once had, but this time with the knowledge and the experience that came with the relationship. Given the right approach, every step away from your partner can be a step towards a new and better relationship, with yourself or with another.

Jeremy and Sarah began the process of splitting up when they came to one of our workshops.

> All the exercises we did seemed to show us that we wanted different things from life, that the demands we made on each other were in total conflict. After the workshop itself, we went back and talked for hours. Eventually, we decided that as a first step, we'd stop sharing the flat together. And somehow, once we did that, we moved apart. (Jeremy)

The best strategy for splitting up is by mutual agreement. Jeremy and Sarah came to the same decision at around the same time, and mutually moved towards the same point — ending.

The leaver or the left?

It's not always so obvious. Usually one or other of you wants to split, and the other doesn't. So there are two possibilities — you are the leaver, or you are the left. Either way, it can be hard. 'Even though I was sure I was doing the right thing' says Paul, 'I hesitated for months before leaving my wife.' The key, once you are sure, is to decide what you want and do it.

Decide, in fact, what it is you want for yourself, and what it is you want for your partner. As the initiator, you can be in control, and if it's important to you that your partner is left with self-esteem and support, then you may be able to help. But also be clear what you want for you, and take it. So often fleeing partners, crushed with guilt that they have dared to seek a better, more fulfilled life, leave ransoms of children and property. You don't need to. You are allowed to be happy as well as free.

So what do you want for you? Is it to leave — that rock-hard certainty that comes, not in the middle of a row when staying seems like giving-in, but in the cool, sad light of the aftermath? If saying goodbye is one way of saying help, or another way of playing murder, then it may be terrible, all mind-changing and re-unpacking, full of strong emotion that is half about going and half about staying. But if you are sure, without a doubt, that a future with this person is going to be a hopeless future, then you can begin your journey without any of the diversions along the way.

How do you leave?

How to leave? It depends what you want for you and your

partner. If you know that the worst possible thing for him is to make love and then break the news, then don't do it, unless you want to maim. If you know that long scenes will leave you feeling drained and desperate, then give yourself a timed five minutes and then walk out. If you need to really talk things through, give yourself a timed five hours. 'We went out for a meal to end our relationship' says James 'We both agreed that it was the right thing to do. Our friends thought we were mad.'

There may well be people thinking you are mad, in the present or in the past, simply because you are getting out. If you find leaving hard, it may be because of the firm messages from your past that leaving is cruel. 'And she walked out on him, the bitch', 'He ditched her, the bastard'; or even earlier 'Mummy won't leave you', 'It's all right, Daddy's here'. And particularly if Mummy did leave, or Daddy wasn't there, you may remember the sickening feeling of being left, and cringe at the thought of inflicting that on someone whom, a while ago, you loved.

If you still love your partner, maybe you shouldn't be leaving. If you don't, which is the kindest act — to stay and give him and yourself second-best for the rest of your life, or get out and give him and yourself a chance of something better? If you are haunted by past or present images of people telling you you should stay, imagine them being in your position with all the information, all the hurt, all the fear that you suffer. Would they stay — and would you admire them if they did?

What you may feel is concern. If the relationship has drifted unvitriolically to a standstill, you may care about your partner's feelings. But beware the 'compassion trap'. 'I was so concerned that he wasn't hurt in the break-up that I agreed to a regular arrangement to see him once a week,' says Rod 'It was only afterwards that I realized how put-upon I felt.' For in the aftermath of a relationship gone sour, you may compulsively try to sweeten it, putting yourself under a strain you don't want, and will eventually break out of it at much more cost to yourself and your ex-partner.

There are other ways. Good friends are usually ready to help, and you can ask them to. 'When we decided to split, I actually went round to most of our friends, told them what was happening and suggested that Jill needed support,' says Tim of a recently ended affair. 'They were great.' Also great, particularly if your partner's grief is too much for them or anyone else to bear, are the professionals; trained therapists and counsellors who will happily take the brunt of caring for the desolated partner while you and everyone else are getting your breath back. And you can, if you are very sure that you are not raising the spectre of false hopes, take some of the brunt yourself, being there as your partner realizes that you're not going to be there for ever, helping her redefine the relationship as a friendship by acting as a friend.

Negotiating a future
Perhaps the most helpful thing you can do, apart from being very clear about leaving, is to be very clear about what happens after you leave.

> When I split with Shaun, we actually sat down and worked out how our relationship would be in the future. We talked particularly about what would be different — we wouldn't be sleeping together, we wouldn't have as much contact. We also talked about what we each expected from the relationship — that we would still see each other from time to time, that we would send cards on birthdays. It made me feel more secure, to know what was going to happen. (Tricia)

If you can summon up the courage to negotiate the ending of a relationship as well as you might have negotiated the start, then you are getting the best for both yourself and your partner.

The exploration will help you do this, by finding out what your side of the negotiation should be. What do you actually want your relationship to be after parting — no contact at all, or a regular uncommitted affair? What do you want (rather than think you ought) to give to your partner, and what do you want to take from him — an evening a month, access to the children, or regular letters? Before talking to your partner, go through the exploration. Explore your worst fantasy and your best fantasy of what could happen, and then write down a realistic hope of what you would want to negotiate. (We haven't included the financial side of breaking up, as this can be a highly complex issue.)

When your needs clash with your partner's needs, you may well need some good negotiation, at a time when you feel anything but good. If she wants to 'keep in touch' when the only thing you want is to forget, then you have to be careful about meeting both your needs in a way that doesn't hurt. But you may also get some nice surprises. Joe discovered, when negotiating a post-relationship relationship with Gwen, that they both wanted a friendship. They felt that simply meeting for a meal regularly might remind them too much of what used to be, so they settled for beginning a brand-new activity together. They took up sailing, which allowed them to spend occasional days together, but in the company of friends, and keep in the sort of touch that was neither shallow nor too intense. A successful ending.

If you are being left
Far more difficult to turn into success is the ending that you don't want. The realization, be it a bolt from the blue or the slow dawning of awful realization, that the person you wanted so much doesn't want you can be one of the most annihilating experiences in the world.

There are some things you can do to stave off the annihilation. Perhaps the first, before you even start to recover alone, is to negotiate what your future together will be like. The strategies that work for those doing the leaving will also work for you. You too have a right to the future relationship you want with your ex-partner, as long as you realize that she does want to be ex, and that chasing after her will only result in her running away — faster.

So negotiate for what you want. For Joanna, it was really important that she got space on her own for a while, to get over David, but then that she had the opportunity to meet him as a friend. They negotiated quite precisely and decided on a period of three months of no contact, and then a tentative drink together. 'He walked in, and I just didn't feel anything but interest — no big emotional hit. Now we meet from time to time, and enjoy each other's company.' For Neil, lots of initial support was important, and his ex-partner Diana felt unable to give this. Together, though, they drew up a list of people who might be able to help, and Diana also arranged to ring Neil once a week to keep in contact. This was an arrangement that took him some way towards what he wanted, without oppressing her.

What if your partner won't negotiate, and reacts with horror and scorn to any suggestion that you can work towards a relationship that suits both of you? If this is so, check out your own motives, for partners who are leaving can smell at a thousand yards any hint of attempts to bar their way. If your suggestion of an impartial drink has the hidden motive of an impassioned reunion, then maybe your partner is merely protecting his own back. But if he really refuses to negotiate, when negotiating means genuinely working through to a solution which will oppress neither you nor him, then think seriously about whether you want to spend any time at all grieving for someone like that.

Think about yourself

Once you have parted, your time is far better spent on yourself. For too long you have probably been concentrating on someone else, who has taken your attention off work, and your mind off life. 'It's difficult to care whether you've washed your hair when you've spent most of the night rowing' as one of our workshop participants once said, and you may well find yourself, leaver or left, in a ground-down state. If you can look around at what you have — money, far too much free time, friends, activities — you can begin to channel a few of them your way. Perhaps you can spend money on you, on things that you choose without having to check out whether your partner approves. Perhaps you can spend some time on you, going to films you like and he didn't, playing sports you like and she hated. There may be friends you can lean on, but tell them to tell you when they've had enough. Everyone may love a lover, but most people will care for an ex-lover too, given the chance to help.

Emotionally, a break-up is among the top ten most stressful things. When someone you love dies, you go through a mourning sequence of denial, anger and finally acceptance. The same can happen when partners break up. There is denial that this is happening, anger that your partner is leaving, and finally — though sometimes not at all — acceptance that it is over. All of this is very stressful. 'I reckon it took a year before I stopped crying,' says Tom, 'and about another year before I stopped yearning.'

You can shorten the process, for you don't have to yearn. The thoughts you have, and the feelings you have about the thoughts, can be changed. The regret you feel is about lost futures, and if you can change the futures to something else, then you will slowly cease to regret. The grief is about the loss of someone you valued, and if you change the value of that person in your mind to being less important than what you are doing at present, then you will gradually cease to grieve.

What did you learn from your relationship?
Think about your relationship. Remember the good times and the bad times. You will probably see pictures of them in your mind as you remember each, and there are likely to be certain key pictures that stay in your mind. You can step outside these and look at what happened, not from the inside through your eyes and your emotions, but from the outside. See yourself, see your partner — but see it all from the vantage point of across the room, or outside the car. Notice these people talking, screaming at each other or crying. Notice how they look, how they sound. By seeing it all from the outside, you can step outside the feelings too, and begin to feel better.

And ask yourself what you learned from all this. Close to, it may not be easy to realize that everything that happened in your relationship has taught you something. At first, you may not be able to understand what that something was, but if you think back again to each incident that is important, seeing it from the outside as before, what you learned from it may become clear.

For we do learn, every time we love. Some of what we learn is helpful — that we can sustain a deep and intimate relationship, that we are good in bed. 'I'll never forget getting a red rose the morning after a particularly lovely one-night stand,' says Eve 'It told me I was special.' Some of what we learn is not so helpful — that we are capable of screaming with hate, that our partners found us boring. It is possible to take with us the good messages, and leave behind the bad ones. And it is possible to choose a partner, next time, who will help us avoid the mistakes we made this time.

The next exploration we offer is a variation on the one at the very start of the book. In Love Strategy 4, we invited you to look at what you wanted from a relationship. After the experience of another partner, your ideas may well have changed, or become more stable.

Look back over the relationships you've had. List out your previous partners. How are they similar? How were they different? Most importantly, are the similarities things you actually want from a partner? Tanya kept ending up with men who depended on her for support and for money. Jim kept meeting women who began by dominating, then complained about having to take responsibility. If you don't want the same kind of person again and again, how come you keep going back to them? How do you need to change in order to avoid making the same kind of mistake?

And now, with the benefit of hindsight, what sort of partner do you want next time? It may take a while before you are ready for next time, ready for the mixing of two minds that demands strength as well as vulnerability. It may take a while before you can even think of that, but when you do, what will you go for? Fill in the chart, taking into account what you've learned throughout this book, and taking into account the patterns of partner choosing that you are now aware of.

With the knowledge you've gained from your last relationship, the chances are that next time round will be more successful than this time round. You may feel that you have lost faith in other people, or even belief in yourself, but in fact having survived at all — let alone with enough awareness to buy and read this book — you enter the next partnership with far more selling points than you entered the last one.

We tend to see endings as destructive. We speak of 'splitting' and 'breaking'. It isn't like that for the dividing cell, which splits and breaks endlessly as it creates new life. So rather than seeing your division from your partner as the end, try seeing it as a creative beginning.

Fig. 16 LOVE STRATEGY 15 Exploration 1

When you split up, what could your relationship be like?

	Worst fantasy	Realistic hope for negotiation	Best fantasy
Time commitment			
Space commitment			
Activities shared			
Social life shared			

Fig. 17 LOVE STRATEGY 15

	Worst fantasy	Realistic hope for negotiation	Best fantasy
Sexual commitment			
How you would relate			
Other			

Fig. 18   LOVE STRATEGY 15 Exploration 2

	Past partner 1	Past partner 2	Future partner 3
Age			
Sex			
Physical appearance			
Mind			
Personality			
Emotions			
Achievements			
Skills			

Fig. 19 LOVE STRATEGY 15

	Past partner 1	Past partner 2	Future partner 3
Job			
Living situation			
People			
Leisure patterns			
Things I valued/ could value about this person			
Things I disliked/ could disliked about this person			
Things I liked at first then disliked			
Reasons we split up			

9.

How do you create futures?

Long-term relationships are not the same as short-term relationships. There are different problems, different opportunities. Some of the people we talked to were happy that their relationships were short-term, but many were aiming for a more long-term commitment. The oldest couple we spoke to had been married for forty-three years.

So what are the particular issues around making a relationship last? They seem to be divided into three; goals, commitment, and a particular change in feeling and approach that makes a couple act, not so much as two separate people, but as one.

Love Strategy 16 looks at setting goals for the relationship, whether that is for next month or for the next twenty years. There is a certain skill in setting goals that both of you want and which will make the relationship right for you in the total context of your lives.

Commitment of various kinds is the subject of Love Strategy 17. Whether that commitment is to buying a house or having a child, to devoting yourself one hundred per cent to one person or to developing a free and open relationship, the promise of commitment is a challenging one.

If you are to turn a working partnership into something special, it is important to build good feelings constantly. Love Strategy 18 looks at how relationships can go onward and upward.

LOVE STRATEGY 16

Establishing goals for the relationship
All seems to be going well. The journey that is your relationship

is continuing. You have survived the first days, holding your breath from one phone call to another. You have lived out the first weeks of dates increasing in regularity and intensity. You have made love, or decided that for you, not sleeping together is the most loving thing to do. You have talked and kept silence, laughed and cried together, negotiated the big issues and circumvented the small ones. You look back at the hills and valleys along the route you have travelled, and see how far you've come. You're beginning to be sure of your partner, and certain of yourself. It's going all right. What now?

Now you can begin to think of the future. After so long attempting to live in the present, and maybe reconciling the past — past lives, past lovers — you look ahead a whole month, or half a year, and imagine your partner still there. And when she talks of Christmas, or he has to organize his holidays from work, it's taken for granted that you will be around.

Planning a successful future

We found that successful couples think about successful futures. They not only look ahead long and hard and plan to include their partners. Their plans are of successful things, activities they both want to do, places they feel it would be good to live in, lives that will be successful, and will be together.

We're not talking about forever. A successful relationship can be a glorious one-night stand. But whatever the future is that you want together, be it an ecstatic breakfast or a happy retirement, one way to make your relationship really effective is to get a clear picture of a future that will work, and head for it.

Notice we say 'head for it'. You don't have to reach your original goal; it might become irrelevant. If we imagine a relationship as a journey again, we can see that directions change. At 50, Jon retired from the police force, bought a boat, and he and Ruth set off for the Med, to do charter work. It wasn't what they'd originally planned, but it did fit with the ideals they'd had when they married — to be together and have adventures. Different destination, same direction.

So if you decide on a future direction for your journey — this hill, that mountain, this marriage, that affair — then you can always change destination if it starts to feel wrong. This marriage, but two children, not four. That fling, but nightly, not weekly. The important thing is to find a general goal that feels

LOVE STRATEGIES

right for both of you, that is good enough to energize you to go for it, and to be flexible enough to change at every step along the way.

If you head for that mountain, you won't know the right route at first. You'll simply head up the nearest hill, in the general direction. At the top of the hill, with the extra perspective, you'll see the next step — on to the next hill, and then look again. And so on. If you set up a future that inspires both of you, you set up the conditions for working together on the first stage of achieving it, and then you'll find out what you have to do next.

> That first Christmas, we started talking, fantasizing really, about our ideal living situation. We worked out the place that would satisfy us both, a perfect fantasy of huge living area, sunken sleeping area, loads of hidden cupboards, and white everywhere. The White Room, we called it. It inspired us for ages, long enough to find a flat, knock down some walls and paint it. The end product was smaller, less plush, and more pale pink than white — but it was what we wanted, and by the time we had it, we had worked out how our life in it would be. (Sue)

The exploration we offer you here is to help you find out how your relationship can develop by imagining yourself in the future, looking back on your past life. If you know that success in your partnership is going to be a short-term relationship, then alter the exploration accordingly. Love need not be for life, and if you are both agreed on that, then success will follow. A word of warning, though; if you and your partner do this exercise, and then discover that the time-scales you are talking about differ dramatically, take care. 'I always thought of our relationship as a long-term thing; it came as a bit of a surprise when, after two years, Michelle announced that she'd always seen it as ending when we left college. I had to come to terms with that before I could really enjoy the time we had left.' says Roger.

Reaching your goals

Time-scale agreed on, and the irrelevant time sections of the grid ignored, begin at the last one, the one furthest into the future. 'We see ours as a retirement relationship' say Nicki and Rob, both in their fifties. 'We set our goals accordingly.' So begin at the end, the furthest mountain you want to head for, and set your goals for that. Fantasize your best future.

Fantasy is the operative word here. To start with, don't be

bound by reality, or by what other people think you should want from life. Begin at the end of your relationship, with the future you feel you really want. Do you really want to retire to a South Sea Island (we do!) or end up with fifteen kids and a dog (someone else did)? Write it down. As you work through the exploration, and get nearer to today's reality, your goals will naturally become more realistic.

You can learn a lot from finding out what you want out of your relationship. You can discover, as Sue did, that you're not as sure as you thought you were that you never want children — because they mysteriously pop up as part of your life later on. You can realize, as Martin did, that you do want to get married as you always thought you did — but maybe not yet. You can find out far better which areas are blissful, and which are not so satisfactory, when they are extrapolated into the future. You may not mind him hogging the phone line with his computer for hours at a time — until you imagine that happening for the next forty years, and decide to renegotiate now.

You can learn even more, and do even more for the relationship, by finding out not only about your goals but also about your partner's. What do you both want out of life? What do you both want to avoid? And, most importantly, do they match?

> I've been out with a number of people, and come to grief because our long-term aims just weren't the same. I'm actually not interested in house and family, but in doing well at work and getting a really exciting lifestyle. When I met Julia, we just seemed to click. She's never wanted children, and is really committed to her job. About a year after we met, I got a vasectomy. That just about summed it up for me — that we were heading in the right direction at last. (Michael)

For love, as the old proverb says, is not about two people looking at each other, but about two people both looking in the same direction. And if you are doing that, and it's a direction that motivates and excites you, then you'll support each other without end, putting up with incredible hardship, emotional and physical, to get what you both want. Phil and Rose took on two ramshackle houses, one after another, and lived in building-site conditions for five years. 'We knew that buying cheap and doing up was the only way to get the house we wanted, so we did it. Now it's all over, we can start a family knowing they'll live in lovely surroundings.'

Common goals, then, can make heroes of us all. Mismatched goals can make tragedies. There can be nothing more soul-destroying than getting to the end of your relationship — or your life — and realizing that all the effort and the heartbreak has given your partner exactly what he or she wanted, but given you only the satisfaction of being there at the time. It may be enough — it is for many 'traditional' wives. But it might not be.

Check your ideas
Checking up at regular intervals can avoid later disillusionment. If your idea of commitment is marriage and she finds this trapping; if your idea of heaven is a commune and she finds this horrifying; if your idea of bliss is a nine-to-five job, and he secretly wants you to aim towards freelancing, then you need to take action.

The action you take can vary. Ultimately, you can part. Couples who love being with each other and get on great in bed have been known to come to grief because their goals just wouldn't fit. But before that drastic step, there can be a wealth of discussion and negotiation. Remember that if you have come this far, you have an inbuilt advantage over couples who negotiate the beginning or the end of their relationship. You have already said you want it to work. You have bright futures in your mind's eye. And if it takes a few hours or days of negotiation to fill in the detail on those bright futures, and make the detail acceptable to you, then you'll do that.

Notice again that we're not necessarily talking about negotiating kids or retirement homes. Getting common, motivating futures is just as vital if you are looking to the short-term, as Helen and James are: 'We see the relationship lasting a year, and we plan for that.' An idea of what you'll be doing next week is a reassuring feeling, and an enthusiasm for this year's summer holiday together is what keeps quite a few couples going through the long cold winter.

So discuss and negotiate. Keep at it until you have some future plans that enthuse you both. If you can't agree that the relationship will last a lifetime, at least talk about the houseboat you'll both live on during the next decade; and if you feel a future of six months is doubtful, then at least decide, in glorious technicolour, which film you'll go to next week. 'I can't see more than a year ahead in any detail anyway,' says Melinda of her relationship 'so in planning our life together, we talk in broad terms. The things we want five years ahead have to be considered very generally indeed!'

Getting the best you can

Once you've got your general future plans, be more realistic. You want a flat together? How are you going to get it? If you can't get the ground-floor flat overlooking the river that you want, what can you get? Our White Room was neither as plush nor as expensive as the original idea, but we knocked a few walls down and added sixteen gallons of emulsion to get a near approximation. What will your near approximations be like?

What do you need to add to the glorious mix that is your relationship, in order to get these approximations? Maybe money, maybe time. Maybe friends to come and help paint, maybe colleagues who will encourage you to go for promotion. Tom's bank manager was quite happy to give him the money for a five-week round-the-world trip with Dave, and Colin and Shirley's accountant gave them some contacts to help them go freelance. If it's information you need, find a resource pack, or a course. If it's confidence you need, do some assertiveness training.

The exploration we offer you next helps you get into the frame of mind which will start you off towards achieving your goals. You need to get together with your partner, probably having done the previous exploration, and having agreed on several goals that you have in common. Write them down on the chart.

Then write down as many ideas as you can think of about how to reach your goal. Brainstorm for a while (even mad ideas allowed) on where to go, who to ask. Totally impossible thoughts can lead to realistic solutions. When Sue and Ian 'brainstormed' the goal of having a home that ran itself, one of the impossible thoughts was to employ a butler! The realistic solution was to have a home-help, who valued the employment while solving the problem. So once you've brainstormed, consider which are the realistic solutions in your situation.

Then think about your resources, what you've got going for you which will help you towards each goal. See your partnership as a whole, so if one of you has woodwork skills, that's something both of you can draw on, and if one of you has a good sense of timing, both of you get to benefit.

Fig. 20   LOVE STRATEGY 16 Exploration 1

Future	Where you live	Life style	Work	Personal growth	How you relate to each other
Fantasy of a best future					

Your own time-scale (decades, years, months)

Fig. 21 LOVE STRATEGY 16

Future	Where you live	Life style	Work	Personal growth	How you relate to each other
Realistic possibilities now					

Your own time-scale (decades, years, months)

Fig. 22 LOVE STRATEGY 16 Exploration 2

	Goal 1	Goal 2
Goal agreed		
Possible ways to reach the goal		
Resources you still need		
Resources you still need		
Where and how to get those resources		
The first step		

Fig. 23 LOVE STRATEGY 16

	Goal 3	Goal 4
Goal agreed		
Possible ways to reach the goal		
Resources you still need		
Resources you still need		
Where and how to get those resources		
The first step		

Money may have to be coped with differently if you haven't yet negotiated a joint income, but negotiating how to cope may be an interesting exploration in itself. After this, consider which resources you still need, and brainstorm again on where and how to get them.

The final step in this exploration is that, for each goal, you decide on the first step. So many wonderful plans have ended up filed under 'D' for Defunct simply because they seemed too big to achieve. Realising what the first step on the road will be allows you to start off without being frightened. Then, and only then, turn your attention on to the second step, and so on.

Step-by-step seems the best way to run a successful relationship. You need to negotiate carefully which mountain you are heading for, because it needs to be one that compels you both forward, seeing clearly that this is a direction that excites and motivates you. Then you can set off, changing direction where necessary, taking detours as you want, realizing when you reach the top of this hill that in fact it is that hill you now what to head for. Step by step.

LOVE STRATEGY 17

Committing yourself appropriately to the relationship

What is commitment? When we asked this question, of couples we talked to, of people we met, we got as many answers as there were individuals. For Terri and John, it was marriage. For Beeda it was having her husband's children. For us, it is at present committing ourselves to working and living together. For Dave it is 'being with and making love with Tom — but I don't demand a long-term future'.

It seems that commitment can vary from the commitment to spend the whole of one night together to the commitment to spend the rest of your life together. The one common factor is that commitment is about futures.

> If I can decide to do something in the future and feel totally happy about it, then I feel I'm committed. I imagine being with Sue in the future, and feel really good about it. That's how I know I'm committed to her. (Ian)

Futures are not now, so how do you know what they will bring?

You have no crystal ball, and no way of telling whether the relationship will be fortunate or not. The answer is that no, you don't know — and that is what commitment is all about. Not knowing whether your future together will bring sickness or health, riches or poverty, yet still deciding to stay — for the summer you are together or the possible three years it can take to get a divorce. That is commitment. Making the picture in your head, imagining the words that will be spoken, and feeling totally positive about it is all you can do.

And many people do it. For Joe, it was imagining Katie being his wife and feeling good about that. For Phil, it was having 'a deep trust about the way Rose will act in the future'. For Liz, it is not being able to 'imagine anyone else who could put up with me except Kathy'. All of them create a future in their heads and feel good about it, and so stick with it.

Starting to commit yourself

There are many outward signs of this sticking with it. Going out together or 'courting' is one. And how do you decide whether to go out with him again, whether to commit yourself that little bit more to a relationship, but by taking what you know, projecting it into a future you don't know, and feeling good about that? For many people, the next commitment is engagement, the formal sign of deciding to marry. Notice how society allows us time to play around with the idea of a future, pretend to be married for a while, and see how that alters the pictures, and the feelings. Some people go a stage further and live together, taking on the commitment of involvement in money issues. Some people go even further and have children together, trusting that for sixteen years at least, they will be happy with the way things are.

Marriage is society's way of formalizing commitment. Though horribly many end in divorce, most people are convinced enough to stand up in front of Auntie Maisie and the lads from the office to proclaim that they are going to stay together until death them do part. And strangely, just doing that can be enough to make the future seem more certain, more attractive.

> After we got married, all my feelings were confirmed. I'd wondered whether I'd feel terribly trapped, but in fact, I was more relaxed, more able to take the rough with the smooth, more able to see us together in the future. (Terri)

And in the years to come, that ability to take the rough with the smooth will be important. For it is this sense of the future and what it will hold, this sense of having promised to spend the future together, which keeps many relationships stable even when the going gets tough. 'When we are rowing' says Ian, 'I think of the future I hope we'll have together, and I can bear what's going on, and stay.'

For there may be things that need bearing, crises inside the relationship, crises outside. Money and tempers may be short. All the difficulties of two people trying to act as one may divide, not unite. And the pictures fade, and the decision — the commitment — can get revoked.

Keeping to your commitment

How can you avoid this? Avoiding crisis is one way, and many other strategies in this book suggest how. The other way is to make sure at the start that the commitment you make is the commitment you will be able to keep.

A commitment that has the best chance of being kept is the one that is easy and natural, the one that has no second thoughts because there is literally nothing better you can do. Not the unthinking rush, but the stop-to-think that brings no second thoughts, no conflict of interests. 'As I walked up the aisle I thought — ah well, there's always divorce —' says Lynn, of marriage to Alex, 'I wouldn't do that again.'

In the long run, it's easier to admit that you're not quite ready for sex, or not quite ready for marriage, than to go ahead and then cope with the problems. Commitment is about looking ahead and feeling good, not about looking around and thinking 'I'd better or he'll think I'm frigid' or 'I'd better because the reception's booked.'

There may well be questions running through your mind, worries about the future, fears about the past. If there are, you need something more. It might be more information, about your partner and what living together might mean. It might be more skills in coping with a family or coping with yourself. It might be more resources, money to pay the mortgage on the flat or an accountant to help you sort out the income sharing you want.

It could be that you need commitment from the other person. Or you might not. Many people are happy to commit themselves without a parallel promise.

If Sue told me she wanted to leave, I'd still want to work on the relationship. I'd want to even if even if her feelings had changed. I don't know how long that would last for — or how it would be if we split up after lots of rows. (Ian)

Others turn off their feelings as soon as their partners' devotion fades. And why not? If what you need is someone to love you as well as someone to love, why not alter your feelings to match theirs, and leave yourself emotionally free to find love elsewhere? Conversely, if you get what you need by feeling your feelings, and you don't need emotions in return, that's fine too.

What isn't fine is when one of you needs what the other can't give. This is why affairs with already-marrieds can be so heartrending; while you are making hopeful pictures of the future together, your lover's lack of pictures can only tell you that your visions won't come true. The same agony can take place if you are the one without the pictures, when through no fault of anyone's, you think of the future and feel bad, or see yourself with someone else and feel better. Knowing that your partner, whom you love dearly for now, will only be truly happy with your love in the future can be a heartbreak too.

Perhaps the only thing to do here is something which may be doomed anyway — to try to change the pictures. Ask yourself what you (or your partner) would need in order to see a better future? What further needs could be met, what projects planned, what interactions changed, for things to look brighter? For further hints on this, turn back to Love Strategy 16, but remember that if you really don't fit together now, then perhaps parting is the best thing anyway.

Exploring your commitment

The exploration we offer you is about commitment. It looks at where you are now in your relationship or potential relationship, and what you need to change your level of commitment one way or the other. This can show you — and your partner — the direction to go in order to strengthen the relationship. It can also provide valuable warning lights to what could threaten it. Even deeply committed couples can benefit from this exploration, which shows you the parameters of where you are at present, and where you want to be in the future.

Consider the commitment you have now, be it to a weekly

date or a lifetime's love. There may be many things which could mean that your commitment will change. Things which you do, like deciding to go abroad; things which your partner might do, such as being unfaithful; things that might happen from outside, such as one of you having to move with your job. Mark down on the chart as many things as you can think of that would reduce the commitment you have. Her dyeing her hair red? Him getting the sack? 'I think I would change my commitment if Caroline had an accident which took away her intelligence. I wouldn't feel it was the same relationship then.' says Pete.

Now think of what would increase your commitment. More time, more money? More commitment from your partner? A change in your ability to handle things? If she had your baby, if he stopped drinking? What would make the difference for you?

Once you've done the exploration, talk it through with your partner if you can. Compare notes on what commitment you already have, and maybe even what commitment you would like to have further on in the relationship. Then share what you have found out about increasing or decreasing your commitment. What do you learn from your partner about her fears or her needs? What can she learn from you? And what does it tell you about how to act, how to love, how to direct the relationship in order to get the level of involvement you both want. Remember, too, that outside factors, such as getting pregnant or losing your job, can be 'insured against' in a number of ways.

The point is that relationships aren't a matter of chance. You may not be able to gaze into a crystal ball and predict the future. Maybe you cannot promise that the commitment you make now will be the one you are able to make for the rest of your life. But you have something better than a crystal ball; your own ability to communicate and to act. For if you can communicate with each other the needs and wants you have, and if you can act to increase your commitment and involvement, then in fact you don't need luck in your relationship!

Fig. 24 LOVE STRATEGY 17 Exploration

	Things that would decrease your commitment	Things that would increase your commitment
Things you might do		
Things your partner might do		
Things that might happen to you (e.g. no choice)		

LOVE STRATEGY 18

Onward and upward

You've fallen in love. Maybe easily, maybe with some pain. You've allowed another person into your life, maybe as far as sleeping together, maybe as far as living together. You've worked through the main issues, worked out just what you each need. You've committed yourselves, one way or another, with promises, with rings, with children. You've forged links that seem as if they're not going to break. So what now?

What now, when the first excitement is over, and you don't think you'll ever be bored? What now, when what was pure good is now a mixture, but is still good enough to imagine staying maybe for life? What do you do with love when it's settled into a happy comfortable existence?

We've talked a lot in this book about the way things can go wrong — differences that need to be resolved, crises that have to be worked through. But most people ultimately find a relationship that works, and when you do — when the differences and the crises have become less important than the bond between you — the question to ask is this. How do you make it even better, and increasingly better? How high can you go? Can you create love more and more as the years go by?

Yes, you can, by using the same spiral effect that causes problems elsewhere in the relationship. For in the same way as you can spiral relentlessly downwards into a break-up, you can also spiral unstoppably upwards into a relationship that is an increasing source of happiness and fulfilment. As we stated in Love Strategy 8, everything we see, hear, do or say can link back to similar things that happened before, be they in childhood or last week, so that you feel the same feelings about them.

Linking good feelings

But these feelings can be good as well as bad. The wonderful thing about links is that they work positively as well as negatively. The way your lover holds you reminds you of being held by a loving parent, and you feel good. The way your lover holds you reminds you of the way she held you last week when you were so good together, and you feel even better.

And good feelings build up the way that bad ones do. Your lover's smile can be wonderful seen across a crowded room for the first time, but how much more wonderful seen for the thousandth time, when it brings with it a million happy memories of times you've seen that smile and been truly loved.

> It seems to get better day by day. I know now that I can trust Phil to be there, so even little things remind me of how much we feel for each other. There's a special phrase he uses when he's pleased or feels particularly loving towards me; 'Oh lovey,' he says. Of course, at first it was just a phrase, but now it's a sign to me of just how strongly he feels. Even thinking of him saying that now makes me happy. It's a special phrase for him now too. (Rose)

For of course links work two ways, and if you feel good, then your partner will pick that up and smile. You'll feel better, linking in that smile to past smiles, and you'll smile too. This is the way love-making often works, from the first drowsy touch to the climatic orgasm, as you each link present pleasure with present and past ecstasies.

Such euphoric links can destroy past horrors, for given enough good feelings to erase the past negative tapes, we can even use our present success in love to give us a new viewpoint on what we always saw as past failures. 'It took me a long while to forget past taunts about my sexuality' says Liz 'but being with Kathy, and feeling good about our relationship, has helped me a lot.'

Finding new links

You may worry when positive links begin to seem common-place. If you are in any situation for long — a dark room or a bright relationship — you can become used to it. But we have some good news for you. Habituation does not necessarily mean that you stop noticing the good things in your relationship. It can mean that you start noticing different good ones instead.

> No, I don't suppose there is the same sense of sheer exhiliration about it all now. But I know so much more about Maria, so much more about what sort of person she is. I've found out things about her that I never even imagined when we met. Like the fact that when we're working together, she has amazingly high standards. She will abandon something without a second thought if she feels it's no good, even if she's worked on it all day. That's something I've come to respect. (Ric)

You can learn to appreciate each other on a deeper and deeper level. The way love is often presented by the media and in books is as the first excitement of romance. Once this is gone, the message seems to be, then all is lost, and nothing remains but to set off into the sunset in search of more excitement. But what we found, talking to successful couples, is that there is a life beyond first love, a life of rows maybe, but also of a deep appreciation of someone as a complete package, their unique ways of doing things and seeing the world.

We didn't find a single couple who had built up only positive links throughout their relationship. What we did find was people who had managed to create enough positive links to make a majority. Talking, doing good things together, love-making (possibly the most powerful positive link in existence), looking after each other, bringing up children — there are a million and one ways you can help yourself and your partner feel good about each other.

Creating love

The exploration we offer you is about creating love. It offers you the opportunity to list out the things you do to make each other feel good — not only the big things such as buying presents and saying 'I love you', but the ones that are more vital because they are less obvious, like expressions and voice tones.

We suggest that you set this exploration up carefully, allowing yourselves time and space, maybe a comfortable setting, maybe a bottle of wine. As you go through, listing out the ways you have of creating good feeling, it may be that the very fact of mentioning them will make you feel good, so be prepared for lots of laughter, hugs, spirals of excitement and euphoria. And be prepared for other things too — more than one couple have ended this particular exploration in bed!

And in the morning, remember that you now have a blueprint for creating your own love, ways of helping your partner feel good about you and about himself. Ask yourself, too, what you can do to increase these chances of euphoria. What links can you build up from the already existing ones, what spirals can you create to add to the ones you've already created?

So if you are happy in your relationship and want it to continue, or conscious that it's already good but want to settle only for the best, then start forging links. Smile by smile, hug by hug, good meal, fun evening, forgiving, giving, gentleness, excitement; working for each other, and with each other, to make it work. And the more links you make, the stronger your relationship will get.

Fig. 25 LOVE STRATEGY 18 Exploration

	YOU	YOUR PARTNER
What is it about your partner that makes you feel just ahhhh . . .?		
How does he/she look?		
What does he/she wear?		
How does he/she move?		
What is particularly important about his/her voice?		
What does he/she talk about?		
Which pet names and special phrases are most powerful?		

Fig. 26   LOVE STRATEGY 18

	YOU	YOUR PARTNER
How does he/she embrace you?		
How does he/she touch or stroke you?		
What's the most powerfully positive memory you share with him/her?		
Of all the aspects of day-to-day living, what's the most meaningful thing about him/her for you?		
What's the most meaningful thing he/she accepts from you?		
What's the most powerful dream of the future he/she can evoke?		
What's the most delightful way he/she can make love with you?		

Now it's his/her turn . . .